Red Flags

Red Flags

*Memoir of an Iraqi Conscript
Trapped Between Enemy Lines
in the 2003 Invasion of Iraq*

AMER FARIS

Foreword by Ibrahim El-Misri

McFarland & Company, Inc., Publishers
Jefferson, North Carolina, and London

FRONTISPIECE: Iraqi cannon stationed among residential buildings. This was a very common scene during the war. Positioning cannons in residential areas dissuaded American airplanes from targeting them for fear of civilian casualties. If the cannons were targeted, the resulting images of destruction could be used by the Iraqi media as evidence of war crimes. All photographs courtesy of Ibrahim El-Misri, used by permission.

LIBRARY OF CONGRESS CATALOGUING-IN-PUBLICATION DATA

Faris, Amer, 1976–
    Red flags : memoir of an Iraqi conscript trapped between enemy lines in the 2003 invasion of Iraq / Amer Faris ; foreword by Ibrahim El-Misri.
        p.   cm.
    Includes index.

    ISBN 978-0-7864-4262-1
    softcover : 50# alkaline paper ∞

    1. Iraq War, 2003– —Personal narratives, Iraqi. 2. Soldiers—Iraq—Biography.   3. Iraq—Politics and government—1991–2003.   4. Hussein, Saddam, 1937–2006.   5. Faris, Amer, 1976–   I. Title.
DS79.764.I72F37   2009
956.7044'342—dc22   2009015400
[B]

British Library cataloguing data are available

On the cover: Iraqi cannons in the desert, surrounded by barbed wire (photograph by Amer Faris); flags and smoke ©2009 Shutterstock

Manufactured in the United States of America

McFarland & Company, Inc., Publishers
  Box 611, Jefferson, North Carolina 28640
  www.mcfarlandpub.com

Table of Contents

PART II: A DIARY OF OCCUPATION

Foreword by
Ibrahim El-Misri

Perhaps we would have been more interested in reading a book written by some general who took part in the U.S. war against Iraq, whether that general was an American or an Iraqi, or from one of the countries of the coalition that joined the U.S. in its military objective of overthrowing Saddam Hussein's regime.

The generals and commanders certainly know a lot of the secrets of this war, or other wars, as they were in positions of command in the fields of war and politics, too, and they participated in shaping these events. But what about a soldier who took part in that war and made it out alive? Is there anything that he can contribute to our understanding of the war? I think so. A huge and significant contribution: not secrets, but an insight into the human suffering when a person is put under tremendous pressure and does not know how to respond to it, or how to ward it off.

Moreover, Amer Faris's book sheds light on other important aspects. What was the condition of the Iraqi soldier during the U.S. invasion of his country? Was this condition one of the causes of the Iraqi army's defeat by the coalition forces? In the context of the Arab world, can a book such as this one help shatter the myth surrounding Saddam Hussein and his army, which ended up into complete surrender, in spite of the ability of the Iraqi man to be a great soldier and true defender of his country and his countrymen? Also, how did the Iraqi military leadership conduct the war against the U.S.? Was it concerned about the protection of Iraq and its people, and the Iraqi soldier?

1

What is striking in Amer Faris's story is that none of the officers in the Iraqi army, especially the high-ranking officers, cared about protecting the soldiers after the fall of Baghdad. Their only concern was to save their own lives while, for instance, the Iraqi soldiers fleeing from the Kirkuk front were facing death from the U.S. forces and the Fedayeen, as related by Amer.

Amer Faris did not hide the fact that he wanted the regime of Saddam Hussein to fall, and he made no secret of his welcoming of the U.S. forces. The fall of Saddam Hussein's regime did not turn him into a supporter of sectarian or ethnic conflict. He was one person among a silent majority in Iraq that distances itself from military, sectarian and ethnic infighting caused for various reasons by local and foreign interests. He focused on the objective which every Iraqi and every human being who has good intentions toward another human being anywhere in the world wants to achieve: an Iraq that is secure, free, cooperative and prosperous.

We share his hopes that his country will become like this, despite all the pains that Iraq has gone through and is going through now. In the end, all humans, whether they are Iraqis or non–Iraqis, know that mutual understanding and common aims and interests, and the rule of law, human rights, and democracy through a transparent electoral process, are the things that bring security, economic prosperity and jobs, and that the fruits are reaped by all. This is what Amer focuses on in his post-war diary.

Amer's book consists of two parts: the first one starts with his brother's execution, and continues with his enlistment in the compulsory military service, the war, and his escape and his return to Baghdad.

The second part is the diary that he wrote from the end of Saddam Hussein's regime until he took the job of interpreter with the U.S. forces in his country, married an American woman, and traveled to America. Both parts are like two mirrors facing each other, reflecting the infinity of human suffering, and sometimes the dreams and happy moments. At the end, these two parts become breathtaking by means of the echoing voice coming from Iraq, which has been subjected to wars and hardships for no reason for a period of thirty-five years, by the Arab Socialist Ba'ath Party and Saddam Hussein, of course.

Amer relates events in a delicate plainspoken manner, with an overflow of emotions regarding his own life and the lives of others. He rarely uses literary styles that hide human suffering beneath piles of

The Al-Karkh cemetery in Baghdad. In the early days of the war Iraqis were able to bury their dead in the Najaf cemetery to the southwest of Baghdad, but this soon became impossible so they began to use Al- Karkh cemetery instead. As the invasion of Baghdad continued, many found it safest to bury their dead near their homes.

words. He knows perfectly well what he is relating as an eyewitness, and not as someone who is watching the war on television comfortably seated on the couch and drinking a cup of coffee or a glass of juice.

I am much obliged to Amer Faris for giving me the opportunity to work with him in telling his story. We worked together for two months almost on a daily basis. Amer was writing and sending it to me via e-mail. I reviewed the dates and the events, and arranged them into chapters with titles taken directly from the text or derived from its context. I did not change anything related by Amer in the book, apart from adding a word or two here and there, or rephrasing some expressions and making corrections related to grammar and punctuation. While he was writing the events of his story, he was like someone who was bleeding, and he had no energy to attend to the formalities of language. His narration flowed gracefully, in simple and expressive words.

We have accomplished a good work mostly due to the efforts of Amer Faris. Let us give him our thanks for having the courage to unveil his painful experience. Should there be any omission or mistake, it is my fault and I gladly take responsibility for it.

Let us listen to Amer's voice, and read this book with a vigilant conscience about man's destiny. The book contains much of the human suffering that we need to see and know. Hopefully, this might help alleviate the suffering caused by the catastrophes, wars and conflicts afflicting most parts of this planet.

—Ibrahim El-Misri is a poet and journalist, who has spent time in Iraq during the course of his work as a reporter.

Preface

Much has been written about the 2003 invasion of Iraq by supposed insiders, and many of these books are valuable accounts of one of the most significant moments in modern history.

While many memoirs have been written by U.S. soldiers from their perspective of the 2003 U.S. invasion of Iraq, to date none have been written from an Iraqi soldier's point of view. The current work, recounting my experiences prior to, during, and after the Second Gulf War, is unique in that it provides the reader a view of those events through the eyes of an Iraqi soldier. My name is Amer Faris and I was a conscript in the Iraqi army.

Across a variety of cultures, from a variety of perspectives, red flags have a distinct and specific meaning. Historically, the red flag is an international symbol for "the blood of angry workers." To sailors out at sea, red flags portend a dangerous storm warning. In the U.S. media, red flags are used as the symbol for danger ahead.

The red flags in my story were more than just demarcation points for placing a cannon aimed at the U.S. invaders coursing across the sky; they were a symbol of my entire existence as an Iraqi soldier. If I stayed on the red flags as I was ordered to do by my leaders, the U.S. fighter planes and lethal bombers would know exactly where to kill me. If I strayed from the red flags, my own officers would execute me, no questions asked.

The same could be said of my induction into the Iraqi Army; upon graduation from university, it was my sworn duty to uphold the government of Saddam Hussein by entering into his army with several years of a required commitment. To not do so was to court execution; to do so was to face an impending U.S. invasion as the hunt for weapons of mass destruction was just then heating up.

Once I was in the military and before the U.S. invasion, our superiors spent as much time guarding us as they did spying on the enemy; it was as if we were prisoners, unable to escape Saddam's oppression even as we fought to keep him in power. Later, during the war, those red flags kept us standing in place as the battle raged on and every impulse told us to flee for our lives.

Even after the war, with the U.S. invasion of Baghdad imminent, we were more at risk of being shot by our men for deserting our posts than we were of being shot by our country's invaders. Our retreat from the front lines, from our air base in Kirkuk through Samarra and back to Baghdad, made us feel as though we were behind enemy lines in our own country.

Red Flags was written first as a diary and second as a testimony to one soldier's survival. Many of my fellow soldiers died during the U.S. invasion of Iraq; many more have died since. Indeed, much has happened since the triumphant days of Baghdad's fall in April 2003; I have watched my high hopes for a successful U.S. occupation of Iraq turn into a chaotic disabling of an entire country.

Much could be said of the politics that led to the 2003 U.S. invasion of Iraq; even more could be said of what has happened since. *Red Flags* is not that story; it is my story. Beyond the headlines, beyond the CNN coverage, beyond even the camera lens I lived the life of a conscript soldier in one of the most lethal and damaging U.S. invasions ever; I survived in spite of the efforts of U.S. soldiers on the ground and pilots in the sky, and despite my own superiors' ineptitude, greed, fear and mounting hysteria.

Red Flags covers the U.S. invasion from start to finish. To an equal degree, it is also the story of what happened after the American invasion of Iraq all the way up to September 2004 and how my hopes came to a sad end. *Red Flags* does not dabble in politics or history; it is the politics of my life during this violent and history-altering invasion—it is my history. In that sense it boils down the headlines, the talking heads, the cross-fires and the political pundits and brings the story home in ways that Americans can recognize. *Red Flags* is unique in that it not only tells an Iraqi's version of the invasion, but does so without the inflamed rhetoric or blinders that dominate many Iraqi versions of this unifying event.

I may have been a soldier in a different uniform, but in many ways

I was just like those American soldiers seen nightly on CNN—just a confused and frightened young man trying to get home to his mother. That my mother lived in Baghdad—ground zero of the U.S. invasion—made my feelings, emotions and recollections no different than if she had lived in Boise, Idaho, or Branson, Missouri. *Red Flags* is a universal story of war and its aftermath.

Beginning in early March 2003 and ending upon my return to Baghdad in early May of the same year, my story spans the entire U.S. invasion. Within those three months a country would fall, another would begin the steep decline into a nation divided by a "war" that would last too long and cost too much, and through it all my life would remain essentially the same.

I was a prisoner before the war; I am no freer now after the war.

And that, I fear, is the invasion's greatest failure

1

Mazin and Ahmed

Despite the fact that many years have passed by since, I can still see that picture clearly in my mind. After having chased his wife and five children away from home, my brother Mazin, forty-five years old at the time, was on tranquilizers and lived secluded in his room on an upper floor. He was completely cut off from the world outside and never talked to anybody. He had a shabby appearance, had grown a beard, and for months in a row, would not take a bath nor change his clothes.

He had the look of a mentally disturbed person. There was no reason after his discharge from the public security prison for his disputes with his wife, save for his worsening psychological condition. His incarceration lasted for more than a year, after which Mazin, who had a dark complexion, came out looking fair and rosy. Perhaps, I thought, his suddenly fair complexion came about because he was kept in solitary confinement, in a cell far away from the sun's rays.

The walls of his upper floor room were as merciless as those of his prison cell. His mental health was deteriorating as the days went by, getting even worse when my mother was there, alone with him. No one in the house knew what conversation went on between them, as they were both careful to keep it secret within the confines of that room.

It would all begin with the crying voice of my mother, and then words would be heard so low that we were unable to make out what was said. It seemed as if my mother was rebuking him, because she always ended with these words, in a loud voice: "Your brother will die like a man, and you will die like a dog." At that moment, Mazin would start to cry. After the ordeal was over, he looked devastated and worn out.

I used to accompany my mother on Tuesdays to Abu Ghraib prison to visit my brother Ahmed. She would bring lots of food because Ahmed always complained of the small amount of food they gave him inside. But, strangely, my mother would also bring stale bread and cheap dates along with her. I asked her, when I first accompanied her to visit Ahmed, "Why do you bring stale bread and cheap dates? And why are you so keen on bringing such low-grade dates?"

She gave no reply. Her eyes were filled with tears. Soon I discovered that she was giving most of the food to the prison guards as bribes, so they would let her bring in the stale bread and dates for Ahmed. The dates were of such low quality that the guards would hand them over to Ahmed and not take them away for themselves. It was then that I learned how resourceful my mother could be.

My brother Ahmed was a young man in his thirties at that time. He had a little girl, and was waiting for a baby, which he asked me to give the name of Farah, should it be a girl. It seemed to me that Ahmed did not care much about his surroundings while in prison. He was always smiling and laughing. The prison did not seem to have had any effect on his cheerful nature. At every visit he asked my mother to forgive Mazin, and in one such visit he told her, "Do not ask him to bear more than what the strongest of men would be able to."

At last, these words of his told me everything: Mazin had been tortured into saying things that led to my younger brother Ahmed's being incriminated. I kept the things I heard in that visit secret, but afterward I naturally had a feeling of aversion toward Mazin.

I didn't know then what it meant to be a prisoner in the public security prison, being inflicted with the harshest of tortures during the day, and spending the night thinking about the plight of your five children when you are thrown into the gloomy places inside that prison.

Little did I know that I, too, would one day find myself in such a prison; tortured in unthinkable ways. Only then would I forgive Mazin.

The secret was no more a secret; to Mazin's great misfortune, my mother's inferences during her conversations with him confirmed whatever my brothers overheard and suspected, and they began to keep away from him, which made his isolation even worse.

A year had gone by after Ahmed was arrested. I was sitting in the living room when I heard a loud banging at the door. It was a distinctive way of knocking—and a familiar one. It would cause fear and anxiety. Immediately I thought, "Maybe they are from the public security, and are here to arrest me, or someone in our family."

Indeed, I heard, "They are from the office of public security." Those were the words of my mother, whispered with a trembling voice and a pale face. As my father opened the door, one of them snapped at him, "Is this the place where Ahmed Faris lives?"

"Yes," replied my father.

"You are requested to report immediately to the public security office."

My father was riveted to the ground. He came back to himself as soon as the security officers were gone, and asked my mother to bring him his walking stick, and accompany him right away to the security department. They both went out, and got into a taxi.

I tried to get control of the situation by reaching there before them. Indeed, I took a taxi, asking the driver to hurry, which he smartly did by going through shortcuts, and I arrived there before my mom and dad. As soon as I got there, I asked to meet the security officer, after telling the guards that I was requested by their officer to come here.

I entered the officer's room. Before I could say anything, he asked me how close I was to, in his words, "the one who was going to be executed." I was shocked, yet I managed to keep my emotions under control and I informed him that I was his brother. He asked me to take a seat, which was more like an order, and I couldn't but execute it without saying a word. He then said to me, in a vengeful tone, "Tea, or coffee?"

He didn't wait for my answer and ordered one of his men to bring tea for the two of us. In a calming voice, he said, "God is most merciful, I want to inform you that—"

I interrupted him saying, "Where's the body of my brother?"

"Wait and do not interrupt me again," said the officer scornfully and went on, "Ahmed has not been executed yet; he will be executed tonight at seven o'clock at Abu Ghraib prison."

As the words began to sink in he then said, "Who told you that the body will be delivered to you?"

I answered with a question, none too eager to give anything away, "Why then did you call me?"

It appeared he was not ready to answer any more questions. Instead he said, "Read this paper and you will know everything, and don't forget to sign it."

And so I read what he handed me:

In the name of Allah, the most Benevolent, the most Merciful
To the family of the criminal who has been sentenced to death, Ahmed:

> The Security Department sends you its greetings and wishes you every happiness. We wish to inform you that your criminal son, Ahmed, will be executed on Wednesday at seven o'clock in the evening.
>
> As such, we would like you to pay him a visit before his execution as you will be able to talk to him. We would also like you to cooperate with us by not holding any mourning ceremony for him. Anyone who goes against this will be held fully accountable.

As soon as I signed that paper, the security officer asked me, "To which party did your brother belong?"

He was not asking this out of ignorance. It was a last attempt on his part to lure me into giving out information that would be used to arrest me. So, I told him, "I don't know. If you can't figure out which party he belongs to, why are you going to execute him?"

The officer was silent for a moment, and then said, "If you, or any one of your brothers try to act bravely, we have enough ropes for you all. Go visit your brother at Abu Ghraib prison!"

I did not comment on what the officer said and remained silent. Not only was I shocked by the news of my brother's imminent execution, I was thinking about my parents and the effect that this news would have on them. They probably would not be able to handle that, and we could lose one of them—or both. As these ideas were spinning in my head, one of the guards at the security department came in saying, "There's an old man and an old woman waiting out at the door, and they're asking to present themselves to you, Sir."

Before the guard could complete his sentence I asked the officer not to let them in, and before he could ask why I told him that they were my parents, and I would take it upon myself to inform them instead of him doing so. The officer agreed, and told the guard to keep them outside until I went to meet them.

Just as I was going out of the room, one of the security officers told me not to bring my parents with me to the prison, because they wouldn't allow us to talk to Ahmed before his execution. He told me that it was a way to torture the executed person's family. They would be sitting in a room that was separated by a glass barrier such that the person condemned for execution would not be able to talk to his relatives, only see them through the glass barrier. Then his executioners would drag him away in front of his relatives. After some time, they would bring the dead body in a coffin. I told myself, maybe this sympathetic soldier was sympathizing with me. When I left the security department, they didn't tell me anything, except some information that they asked me.

I decided not to inform anybody of Ahmed's execution before its taking place, in order to avoid them visiting him at the prison, and being subjected to the horrible situation where they would see Ahmed with his executioners. In fact, I was torn between avoiding that horrible situation that any member of our family might be in, and Ahmed being in need of seeing us before they executed him.

It was a difficult decision, the burden of which I still carry till this moment, with Ahmed reproaching me in my conscience and in my dreams. I returned back home. After a while, my mother came dancing with joy, as she said to me, "My dear boy, fill in this application form."

It was a letter appealing for a meeting with Saddam Hussein in the hopes of getting an amnesty for my brother, who was sentenced to death. I wrote the letter, and accompanied her to the presidential palace, which is in the eastern Karadah region. There, we found dozens of women and children, including old women, waiting at the main gate of the palace. All they received while waiting there was a string of obscenities that the guards at the gate would hurl at them, and beatings with the butts of their guns, and kicking.

As for their letters, they were thrown right in the bins at the gate. I was amidst those people, shoving and pushing away one another, not minding about the guards' kicks. I don't know why I stood there, hour after hour. Was I punishing myself? At one point, I found myself begging a guard to take my application letter for a meeting, although I was completely aware that they would throw it away in the bin.

I suppose I only wanted to give my mother a glimpse of hope that would last for one night, so that she might close her eyes and sleep, as nobody knew how she would welcome the news of the execution the next day. I went back, and my mother was happy thinking that the letter would be on Saddam's desk the next day, not knowing that the letter never left the pocket of my trousers.

The next morning I informed my maternal uncle and my brothers of Ahmed's execution. It was my uncle who told my mom and dad about it. We received the body of my brother, all covered with bruises and injuries, and without any fingernails or toenails, as a result of torture, and we did not let my mother lift the shroud off his face to look at him.

I resumed study at the university four months after my brother's execution. I wished I could hide the fact of what had happened to my family, fearing what persecution I would get at the hands of the party cadre at the university if they knew of this matter. They are no less criminals than the security officers at the general security directorate. The university was as a police foundation seeking to maintain the Ba'athist regime and to protect the dictator.

Two or three days after resuming study at the university, my application was sent to the principal of the department where I was studying. When I talked to him, he told me that he had been informed that my brother was executed, and he needed to ask me some questions about his case. I denied being aware of anything, thinking that he would accuse me of joining my brother's activities against the government. His proof of this would be any word I said.

When I continued denying the facts, the professor had no choice but to ask me to sign a paper stating that I had to keep away from any congregations of students and to stop associating with any one of them so as "not to influence their supporting belief of the revolution and the party." In addition, I was warned not to participate in any adverse activity against the party and told that I would always be on parole.

In fact, I began to keep away from my colleagues and friends at the university. Their curiosity used to push them to ask me about the reason for avoiding them. Therefore I had no alternative but to create hassles with them to force them to keep away from me in order that neither they nor I would be exposed to the anger of the party apparatus. In a short time, I started losing my friends one after the other— and forever. I began feeling a true alienation within the university environment. The study was the most difficult time for me.

In addition to the party apparatus persecutions, the hate of students began to reverberate into aggressive actions and comments. I used to hear such statements as that I was crazy or I was suffering from a mental illness. This explained my recurring fights with them. I used to excuse them for their stand; I tried my best to accomplish this. In fact, I quite succeeded in this. I became the worst person in the university with regard to mood and morals.

Keeping away from the students and self-withdrawal within the university campus reduced my movement and forced me to spend long times on a wood bench in a garden overlooking the building of the party division adjunct to the Ba'ath party. Although nobody asked me to sit there, I was diligent in occupying that seat, just as if I were trying not to hide from the eyes of Ba'athists, thinking that they would think I was deliberately hiding from them to carry out actions against Ba'ath.

Despite the ugliness of being watched in everything I did, sitting on that seat for a long time turned me into a watcher, too. It made me fit to monitor all movements of Ba'ath party members inside the university, analyze them, and know what these movements meant, contrary to the simple state in which I was before resuming my study.

The party cadre, represented in the Saddam students' branch of the Arab Ba'ath Socialist Party, was the only commander at the university. It had the authority to expel students and punish them if their loyalty for the dictator waned. In addition, the youth and students' union was headed by the tyrant's eldest son, Uday Saddam Hussein, who was known for his brutality and belligerence and his lust for women and sex.

The students' union used to include a group of students associated with the Ba'ath party. They were nominated by the party and had won false elections (held in the university) in which all students took part every year. Although the duty of the youth and students' union supposedly was to defend students' rights and facilitate matters related to the study in the university, its actual job was to watch students and to monitor any antigovernment activity by means of the members of the union, distributed into all study departments of the university, who used to tag this-and-that student with false accusations of carrying out suspicious acts to disturb security and order in the university. As a result, they would arrest the student and if he did not "confess" to his "crimes," he was tortured and beaten up inside the union, which is located at the second floor of the university.

Many times while walking that floor I saw the members of the students' union attack a student, hitting him severely until he fainted. This was not the only reason for this room to be at the second floor; it was also used for sexual assault on girls at the university.

At that time, there was a group of female students working for Uday Saddam Hussein at the university, who used to be his mistresses before and after their friends got bored; it was enough for them to work as his pimps inside the university.

Their job was to strike up an acquaintance with pretty students, take their pictures, and show them to Uday later on. If he was interested in one of them, they would tell her that Uday was interested in spending a night with her. Woe to one who refused Uday's invitation.

One of these students was Bayda, who it appears refused to build a relationship with Uday. This led him to employ his despicable means with her and her family. Bayda collapsed in front of the students crying and weeping, after learning that the security forces had arrested her father and put him in Al-Radhwania jail, where Uday used to practice torture and killing.

I do not know what happened to Bayda after that day. She disappeared for a while and then she came back as a different person. Bayda was no longer an innocent, peaceful student. She acted violently, snobbishly, and with hate for everybody around her. She got used to going out with Uday's pimps in Mercedes cars like the ones used by Uday's guards, taking them from the gate of the university every so often.

This was the suffering of the female students who were prettier than the rest. With regard to the rest of the female students the story differs a little; some of them became victims of professors from the authorized party apparatus, especially those girls who made love relations with some students at the university.

The members of the students' union and the rest of Ba'athists monitored lovers inside the university and, if they saw a guy and a girl sitting together by themselves, they would catch them immediately as if the two lovers were criminals running from justice. They claimed that the two lovers were kissing, which was forbidden inside the university.

The mores and conventions do not allow relations of this type, and the lives of the boy and the girl would be in danger if their families heard about it. In such cases, party members or students' union members practiced extortion on both students after they terrorize them, threatening them with the disclosure of the secret of their relationship unless the girl had sex with them. Among those was the reporter of our department, who roamed around hideaway places in the university along with a member of the students' union, hoping to catch lovers for this very reason. I used to see him walking normally, then, as he heard lovers' whispers, he would quickly hide behind a tree and then jump in front of them as a cursed devil.

The image of two lovers insulted in front of the eyes of all in one of the university corridors, by a group of Ba'athists, while the boy begged the members of the union not to inform the family of the girl, remains with me today. Whenever this scene recurs in my mind, I feel the depth of insult that we face as humans in the land of petroleum and blood. Love has become a curse; love has become a crime in my country. The beautiful feelings of lovers have become a gate through which the criminals can satisfy their abject goals.

With regard to professors who were not registered with the Ba'ath party, their condition was miserable. They were deprived of the privileges of their teaching staff-mates. They remained like this until the party leadership issued an order to join all professors to the Ba'ath party. Whoever refused this, of course, was subject to persecution from Ba'ath party individuals until he resigned or left Iraq—or he yielded to their terms. Many of those who had high diplomas at the university had to leave Iraq, among them Professor Hadi, Dr. Hameed, and Dr. Abdulahad, although they did not have enough knowledge to qualify them to become professors at my university. Their eligibility was that they were members of the Arab Ba'ath Socialist Party.

Even the studies at the university began to serve the government and to enhance its authority. The scientific researches of students headed toward what the Ba'ath party wanted. When I submitted the idea of a paper on the dialect of Al-ahwar (marshes) people in Iraq, and the impact of environmental changes on their dialect, my research was refused decisively; the reason, without doubt, was that the party did not want research to disclose crimes of the regime.

Of course, I did not directly bring up the subject of the drying up of the marshes (Al-ahwar), done by Baghdad authorities to eradicate the marshes region and to annihilate the last stronghold of the Iraqi opposition to the dictator. Instead, I tried to deal with this subject in a sensitive way to avoid any pursuit from Ba'ath authorities.

The head of the department changed the topic of my paper, after he threatened to submit a party report on me if I did not desist, asking to conduct an investigation about my reasons for selecting such research. He asked me to do my research on translating Saddam Hussein's sayings. In fact, I was forced to do so, because I was unable to refuse. After all, who is it that refuses to translate sayings of a dictator such as Saddam Hussein?

Meanwhile, I was monitoring with pain how the university corridors became a hotbed for whores, who exposed their bodies for rich students, of course, and members of the party in the university and of the students' union. The regime did not care what these students were doing; on the contrary, they were also security agents building relations with the children of the rich class, who are influential in the government, and they could take every movement and word to the security forces. Of course, the rest of the poor professors were unable to do anything. They were afraid of the power of these whores. I saw with my eyes how one of them who was studying at the college of arts insulted the dean of the college, because he dared ask her to not wear her outrageous clothes and to stop her suspicious behavior. After a while, the

A sandbag barricade used by Iraqi soldiers in the streets of Baghdad. In the first days of the war, the army was providing sandbags for protective barricades, but as the American army advanced towards the city, the Ba'ath party members started to collect bags from the people, apparently as part of a plan by Saddam's regime to engage in a sustained street fight against the American army.

dean of the college resigned, and all were aware of the influence of that whore inside the university.

This was not the only reason for study deteriorating in the university. Study was also irregular due to stupid resolutions from the government including training on weapons, which led to the waste of many hours that should have been used for study and scientific achievement.

The reason was the relationship of the regime with the world society, which is tense. Iraq tried to keep away from the American hammer by allowing the inspection team to search for weapons of mass destruction, but at the same time, it procrastinated and played the cat-and-mouse game. As the government expected to come under an American military strike, the regime was frantic in its attempts to hold out and wait for the U.S. to strike before taking any action. The Ba'ath party called for comprehensive weapon training for all Iraqis, and of course, the regime would not exclude any section of the society, including students.

Therefore, they partially crippled universities; all were subject to training on weapons including university students and professors. The training lasted for a while; we were forced to leave study halls to go to the soccer field at the university. The training was just a stupid lie; what we did was march for hours at the office in order for the party officials to see us in preparation for a show in front of Saddam Hussein. I used to smile secretly and to make fun of this show, and I saw the whores organized in training, too. One of them was walking in front of the students in an outrageous way, while the students reiterated slogans of the Ba'ath party.

I remained in this compulsory training until a moment when I was walking in the front of a picture of the tyrant; the picture was placed on the stage to indicate the place where Saddam Hussein would be during the show. At this time I saw that what I was doing looked like disloyalty to my brother, who had been executed by the regime of this dictator. I was unable to bear this Ba'athist farce any longer and I decided not to continue with the training. I insisted on my stand despite the pressure of my mother's asking me to continue training, fearing that I would become the victim of the violence of the party apparatus in the university. After the show was over the following day, the Ba'ath party in the university expelled those students who did not take part in the show; I was among them. I despaired; I had several months left to graduate. One of the party members stepped in for me after I bribed him; in fact, thanks to him, I completed my school there.

2

111th Battalion, Air Defense Division

I graduated from college and received a degree in English. This certificate could mean a lot to other people, but to me, it meant that a new stage in my life was about to begin, which could be much worse and more painful than the previous one: joining the ranks of the Iraqi army. Therefore, I went to the conscription office so as to avoid punishment that could double my military service period.

A few days after I reported to the conscription office, they informed me that I would be taken to undergo military training on January 1, 2002, and that I had to be present at the office on that date.

There were hundreds of young people present there that morning who were, like me, awaiting their transfer to the training camps. Hours had gone by, when one of the training officers ordered us to gather in the conscription office's courtyard in an orderly fashion, and then said, "How do you think we will face the U.S. offensive, while you are still unable to maintain some order?"

His tone was such that I almost believed him. When we were gathered in the courtyard, I was thinking that we would soon be transported to our training camp. Things turned out differently. The trees in the courtyard were festooned with decorations, and there was a large tent that was set up, with luxurious furniture and fine carpets. The tent was obviously reserved for the officers.

The courtyard was full of soldiers standing, forming the shape of an "L," with the tent sheltering the officers in the third side. I didn't know why they left the fourth side empty. There were many journalists who were taking photos and filming the ceremony of the youths being taken away for mandatory military service. There was a platform, and a commentator wearing a military uniform was standing near it.

While I was watching that great circus, there arrived a bus carrying a group of old women who looked like they were destitute. One of the soldiers approached the bus driver, and angrily said to him, "Why are you late? The celebration is about to begin and the Iraqi TV will be covering the ceremonies."

The driver replied, "It isn't my fault. I had to wait for a long time at the market so as to bring these old women. They wouldn't come for less than two thousand dinars." That was ridiculous to me.

The celebration began, and the women began to dance and clap their hands. When the TV camera turned toward the old women, the commentator spoke at length about how the mothers were so happy that their sons were going to join the Iraqi army. At that moment, I was thinking about my mother and her feelings, and comparing that to these women and what they were paid to do.

We arrived at Attaji camp for infantry training. We had to undergo basic training on infantry skills before being transferred to other branches within the Iraqi army. Attaji camp is located outside Baghdad. It is a huge camp, but it lacks the simplest services. There is no drinkable water, no healthy restrooms; this is what I saw myself.

When there was a need for me to go to the restroom, I tried to find restrooms at the camp, but I could not. I went to the sergeant in charge of training and asked about the location of restrooms. He laughed loudly and said, "This entire wide place around you, and you are asking for a place to poop?"

He was referring to the wide space around him, which has nothing except concrete walls with Ba'ath slogans and empty land, which was the training field. I was amazed. Did soldiers actually poop and pee in the training field? This was the fact of the situation, so I had to handle it. Shortly I saw some trainees walking long distances into the empty land to be as far away from the eyes of other soldiers as they could, to have a kind of privacy while they were relieving themselves.

One of the sergeants took us toward a training field with sincerity and respect. He kindly asked us to walk with him until we got to a wide-spreading field, where we stood close to an officer and the sergeant gave him a paper. The officer began reading our names and then he welcomed us. Pointing to big cardboard boxes he said, "These are Iraqi army uniforms, but you will not wear them now. We will do a simple warm-up with your civilian clothes before we give you these clothes."

He looked balefully at the sergeant and asked to start warm-up, at the time I was wearing my civilian clothes. As soon as the officer finished talking, the sergeant changed his kind tone and began insulting us without reason. We went under a stream of insults to a muddy, marshy region. The sergeant asked us to run around a distant palm tree.

My friend and I were looking at each other wondering about the wisdom of letting us run on the marshy land, but despite this, we ran as much as we could. When we were behind in our running, I was overtaken by the sergeant running toward my friend. He pushed him, at which time the poor person fell in the mud. The sergeant was telling us, "The last five in running will run one more time."

I had to run with the rest of the soldiers, and of course, I was the last one of the joggers. He asked us to run one more time around the palm tree. I was hardly running, since my shoes were not for such warm-up. While I was running my shoe stuck in the mud and it came off in spite of me. I stopped to take it out of the mud. The sergeant called, asking me to hurry up, so I left the shoe and jogged without it. The sergeant kept on sending us around a tree until our legs failed. We stopped on our faces in the mud and, at this time, the sergeant said to us, "Relax a little bit."

The first hours were enough to divide the soldiers into two groups. The first group was children of the rich who were not ready for such miserable situation, I used to see them trying to get close to the sergeant. Among the trainees in the camp with me was a young man called Adnan. He was one of the children of the rich in Baghdad.

I knew him because he was with me at the university. I asked him about the reason behind trying to get close to the sergeant. He told me that he wanted to talk to the officer, to bribe him so that he could leave the camp and never come back again. In fact, he was eventually able to talk to the officer; he took the officer's phone number and left the camp. This was the case of the rich at the camp. Their military service does not outlast the first day. As the sergeant began the hard training and insults, they started getting close to him and paid bribes to get rid of the travail and dishonor, leaving the camp for the second group such as me who could not pay.

Among the remaining trainees were my friends Sinan and Riadh, in addition to a young soldier called Baha, to whom I was introduced. Baha was an orphan and his grandpa had spoiled him; therefore, he was not ready for such suffering. Sinan had the same living conditions that I had. I understand that soldiers must train and obey military orders, but our camp was not like that. It looked like a torture camp. Actually, it *was* a torture camp; the purpose of it was merely to abuse and insult soldiers to get them to the point where they preferred to pay big money to preserve their dignity.

Iraqi society suffers from huge differences between classes, which became worse with the economic embargo. Although I was suffering, I was unable to pay money to the sergeant and the officer. I was obliged to accept their food, which was bread and cheese for both lunch and supper. The first day passed by with running around the palm tree. I laughed to myself, and I wondered what this training was for. Were they preparing the army for another defeat like the one of 1991?

I continued cursing the sergeant in my heart whenever he called us stupid, but I smiled whenever he asked with a glance about what running I had completed for myself. We endured this until night came. The sergeant stopped us and he said to us, "You go now, and come back tomorrow at 3:30 A.M. Have your head shaved by then ... or else."

It was 10:30 P.M. by then, all haircut shops were closed and, in addition, I was completely exhausted. My mother opened the door for me; she looked at me and at my dirty clothes. My sister came to me. She took off her gold jewelry and she asked me to sell it and bribe the officer, but I refused it. I preferred to go on with training. I went to sleep, setting the alarm for 2:00 A.M.

The second day I went to the camp only to find there was nobody except some soldiers and loose wild dogs, the kind which fill the streets of Baghdad at night. I was carrying some cake which my mother had made for me. The dogs, which wanted to attack me, left me alone after I shared the cake with them.

"Even dogs hate soldiers," I grumbled sleepily to myself.

Everyone serving in the Iraqi army learns this philosophy sooner or later. I ascended into the bus going to the camp and found that most of those in the bus were asleep, and those who were awake like me were like those going to execution court. When I got to the camp I was surprised that the majority of the soldiers had had their heads shaved, and the rest had had their hair cut with scissors. This meant that their heads were like stairs of hair. I remembered my hair, which I had not had cut, while standing beside a man who had not had his hair cut either. He said to me, "We might get a free haircut."

We arrived at the training field, where we squatted for two restless hours. Whenever we wanted to sit comfortably, the sergeant punished us with standing up and sitting down for many times until we were satisfied that sitting in such an uncomfortable position was better than being punished by the sergeant. When the first morning light appeared, the sergeants moved among the lines, searching for their victims. The sergeant pointed to me and to the person who talked to me and he asked us to get out of the line.

As we did that he stopped us in the front of the soldiers. He said to the soldiers, "Do you know what these stupid men did?" Then he answered himself. "They did not adhere to the rules, of course, because they are stupid. I'll make them a lesson for anyone else stupid like them." Immediately he took a hair clipper in his hands, asked us to sit down on the floor and began cutting my hair. He did not cut it as haircut, but he left the sides and he made a line in the middle of my head with his hair clipper.

While some soldiers were making fun of us, he asked us to run around the soldiers and shout, "We are stupid." The humiliation did not stop at this point. He took us to a muddy place where the sewage water ran from the only restrooms at the camp, set apart for officers. He asked us to crawl through it. We refused this order. The sergeant immediately walked toward the officer and told him about our refusal. The officer came close to us and asked the sergeants to arrest us and put us in jail at the camp.

This matter did not mean anything to me; by now I had reached the end of my patience. I was not about to accept any more humiliation. The camp jail was huge; there were many private prisoners from those who deserted the military service, arrested by police. They put them in prison until they were taken for trial and, after that, they transferred them to other prisons.

The jail looked like a rear street where types of drugs are sold. The majority of prisoners used drugs continuously. I wondered where they got these drugs inside a military prison at a military camp. Later I learned that sergeants sold drugs inside the prison with the knowledge of the officer, who monopolizes the drug trade. He gave orders to punish prisoners who tried to get drugs via their friends who bring drugs to them concealed in plastic bags with food.

Through a friend of mine, I informed my family that I was in the military jail. I asked them not to visit me after I saw with my own eyes how the guard and the sergeants humiliated prisoners' families. I was very depressed, though I consider myself an optimist, one who can adapt to the environment; but the second experience in jail made me lose faith in the power of my patience.

The difficulties that I faced were almost unbearable. I remained in jail for a while until the minister of defense, Lieutenant General Sultan Hashim, visited our camp. He released all prisoners at the camp. The reason was not that the camp commander wanted to reduce our sentence, but that he was in immediate need of the prisoners to cover for soldiers who had bribed him to stay home. With the prisoners, he could conduct a count and put on a show in the front of the minister.

The overall number at the camp was supposed to be over one thousand, but the actual number did not exceed a thousand. Therefore, the camp commander resorted to a trick I think he had practiced in previous military shows: he would do the show with one division instead of four companies, which were supposed to attend the show.

Each company had a symbol with a specific color—a yellow, blue or violet ribbon in addition to other colors—to differentiate soldiers of each company from other companies. Therefore, the camp commander ordered us, all soldiers in the camp, to wear the blue color first, appear in front of the minister, and be counted. As the commander didn't have enough soldiers and was scared of this being disclosed, sergeants asked us to go to the building of one of the companies, change our ribbons with theirs and appear in front of the minister.

I found this to be a good opportunity for revenge against the camp commander who had put me in jail. I was always walking on the side facing the defense minister. Each time I got close to him I shouted, "Long live the leader Saddam!" trying to get the minister's attention so that he might wonder why this soldier was taking part in the shows of all the companies, but it did not work.

After having spent some time at this camp, I received a letter informing me that I was being transferred to an air defense battalion.

It took us five long hours by bus to make the arduous journey to the 111th Battalion. It was located behind the Northern Gas Company, in the city of Kirkuk, the city to which the Iraqi government migrated thousands of Arab families, while thousands of Kurdish families were forced out in order to create a new demographic reality that would give a rather Arab character to the city. The military assignment of the 111th Battalion of the air defense was to protect the strategic Northern Gas Company, should it be the target of an air strike.

When we reached the gate of the battalion, we were subjected to a tight inspection, after which the guard let us in. As soon as we were

inside, Riyad, Sinan, Baha—these were the soldiers who were transferred together with me from the air defense training center in Baghdad—and me, scrutinized every nook and cranny at that battalion. It
was comprised of several mud-built rooms, and the roofs were made of
tree branches covered with sheet metal.

A small, gloomy room located to the left of the gate caught my
attention. It was isolated, and a board above it read "Battalion Jail." The
room was surrounded by barbed wire, and foul odors emanated from
there. Out of a little window, pale faces would appear, then quickly vanish as the guards at the gate shouted angrily at them. That room was
one of only two rooms that were built with concrete and bricks; not
because the commander of the battalion was concerned about the
inmates inside that room, but out of fear that they might run away. The
other room was for the commander of the battalion. As I was lost in
my contemplation of that inhospitable surrounding, I heard the voice
of Riyad saying to me, "This is the condition of the battalion, and it's
the main compound. How about the batteries and the secondary com-
pounds?"

Despite the harshness of the new location, which seemed worse
than the training camp that we had been transferred from, I tried to
keep a positive attitude by saying to myself, "It's only one year and a
half that I will have to spend here or somewhere else, whether I like it
or not." As for Baha and Sinan, I could see expressions of annoyance
on their faces.

We went toward the open area in front of the commander's room,
the only other room built with concrete and bricks. I stepped toward the
commander's guards standing at the door and informed them that we were
newly transferred soldiers to the battalion, and we had the letter of our
transfer with us. One of the guards took the paper and went to the commander. A minute later, he came back and said, "Go to Master Sergeant
Jiyad's room and he will ask you for some important information."

I felt quite anxious and wondered to myself what kind of information the master sergeant would take from us. Finally, we made our way
to the room, and saw a man in his mid-forties, skinny, bad looking, with
a thick moustache. He had two fountain pens hanging on his sleeve
pocket, which made it clear to me what kind of information he would
take from us, or more precisely, interrogate us about. That particular
style was common to all working with the military secret service.

Baha went in first for the interrogation while we were waiting outside the room. Of all those waiting, I was the most anxious, so much

so that Sinan drew close to me and whispered in my ear, "Don't tell them your brother was executed."

I responded, "Am I that stupid to say such a thing?" Then came my turn, and suddenly I was before the master sergeant, who inspected me closely, perhaps because he noticed that I was anxious despite all my efforts to conceal that.

He asked, "Are you a Ba'athist?"

"No, sir," I replied in a low voice, "I haven't joined the Ba'ath Party yet."

"Why not?" he asked, sensing an opportunity. "Don't you believe in the principles of Ba'ath?"

"I do believe in the principles of Ba'ath, sir. But I couldn't find the time to join the party; I was busy with my studies."

"Even college students should join the party," was his concise reply.

I realized that he was trying to lure me so as to record any slip of the tongue on my part, which could be used to accuse me of being against the principles of the party and the revolution, which he would then report to the secret service and get twenty-five thousand dinars as a reward for having reported a potential enemy of the party and the revolution.

I succeeded in getting things under control as I mentioned a quote from one of Saddam's speeches, saying, "Our President and Leader Saddam Hussein, may Allah's Care and Protection be with him, once said in an address to the nation that everyone is a Ba'athist even though he has not joined the party."

This quote from his speech was sufficient to prevent the master sergeant from luring me anymore. My attempt was successful, indeed. I had previously tried this quote to escape from an interrogation that party members put me through, as to why I had not joined the party during my studies.

The master sergeant kept silent for a while, and then asked me the question I had feared most since coming in front of him: "Was anybody in your family executed, or accused in matters related to politics?"

"No, sir," I answered.

He threw a paper at me requesting me to sign it. It contained specific threats to whoever hid information concerning himself, or who gave false information. I signed the paper, after which he ordered me to head to the food storehouse and tell them that I was a new member of the second battery unit, which was one of the secondary units attached to the battalion.

While we were waiting at the food storehouse, the master sergeants of the battery units came to the person in charge of the food depot, who told them that we were transferred to their battery units. One of the master sergeants, Abu Hisham, moved toward us and said, "Where are Amer and Baha and Sinan? Let them come with me."

I asked, "Are we heading to the battery unit now?"

"Not now," Abu Hisham replied. "First we have to take the unit's share of food."

"Where is the car that will take us there?"

His reply was almost mirthful as he told me ruefully, "You can forget civilian lifestyle. You are now in the military. Or, maybe you want us to bring you a limousine?"

I knew, by that harsh reply of his, that the battery unit did not have any means of transport. So I remained quiet, until he threw a sack at me and said, "You and your friend, open this sack. The man in charge of the food depot will put the battery unit's share in it." Then he handed me a paper, which probably had the number of soldiers written on it.

The man in charge of the food depot said, "What is this, Sergeant Abu Hisham? Your number has risen to thirty-three soldiers?"

"Yes," came the reply, "we have ten newborn babies as a result of the nocturnal activities of the goats."

The food depot person laughed, and ordered his assistant to give us sixty-six loaves of bread and three chickens. Abu Hisham then beckoned us to move. On our way to the battery, we had to take turns carrying the sack. Sinan and I carried it for most of the journey, while Baha walked beside us.

Baha wasn't prepared for life in the military. He was more like a child who needed constant care. Actually, Sinan and I were wary about what could happen to him, especially since he had had a bad experience with the sergeants of the training camp that we had transferred from. If we hadn't intervened at the right time, the sergeants would have raped him. Since that incident, we asked him to accompany us wherever we went, in order to avoid being in such a situation again.

We were walking in a very rough terrain made up of small hills. The sergeant quickened his pace toward the battery unit, always keeping a distance of five steps ahead of us, not heeding Baha's pleas and repeated queries about the remaining distance to the battery.

I asked Baha to carry the sack, while I hastened to reach Sergeant Abu Hisham. I tried to lighten the mood and joked with him saying, "Is it a battery unit or a maternity hospital?"

American helicopters flying over Baghdad. In the initial days of the invasion of Baghdad, American helicopters used to fly very close to the buildings and house-tops.

He looked at me with astonishment, and said, "Why?"

I realized then that maybe he didn't understand what I meant to say. So, I clarified myself, saying, "I heard you say to the man in charge of the food depot of the battalion that ten babies were born to the battery unit."

"Yes, the soldiers of the battery are like goats, they mount on each other's back."

I didn't understand his words, and I didn't want to make my conversation with him any longer, as his reply was not amiable.

After a journey that took us more than an hour, there appeared in the distance a high hill overlooking a little river, and above that hill were four mud-built rooms. When we reached the battery, we found only seven soldiers and a young lieutenant.

The sergeant approached the lieutenant, saying, "These are new soldiers who have been transferred here."

I found the behavior of the sergeant toward the lieutenant quite strange, as the sergeant didn't give the military salute to the lieutenant, and he spoke to him as if they were of the same rank. The lieutenant looked at us arrogantly and said in a self-important voice, "Introduce yourselves."

So, I introduced myself, after giving the military salute. I mentioned, among other things, that I was born in the year 1975.

"So, you are twenty-eight years old. Were you avoiding military service?" the lieutenant asked me.

"No, sir," came my pat reply. "I just graduated from college and joined the army after that."

I couldn't understand why he didn't like me. Perhaps because I was a university graduate, unlike most officers who failed their exams since preparatory school, and whose low grades forced them to join the military college so as to secure a job in the army.

The officer ordered us to go to the main munitions depot and carry the anti-air ammunition for the 75 mm cannon to another depot down the hill. There were more than 400 crates weighing about 50 kilos each. I was expecting him to relieve us of our duties, especially considering the fact that we made an arduous journey to the battery, five hours by bus and one hour on foot in the hills.

Sinan and I had to do most of the work. The time it took us to carry two crates would be the same time that it took Baha to carry one. I also noticed a group of soldiers watching us with scornful eyes while we were diligently carrying the munitions.

I did not know why yet, though I soon would.

3

The Lambs of the Reeds

After a day's arduous work, we heard one of the soldiers shout in the loudspeaker: "The soldiers are requested to gather in the battery's courtyard for dinner." But when we all gathered, there were only nine soldiers and two cooks. One of them prepared food for the soldiers, and the other for the sergeant and the officer.

Hazem, the soldiers' cook, was the weirdest cook I had ever seen in my life. The mere sight of him would make one lose one's appetite. He was a soldier with a long beard, and wore shabby military clothes stained with oil and tomato sauce all over. One could hardly distinguish them from a mechanic's. And I was almost certain that he had not taken a bath for months.

Everything about him showed that he was mentally ill. As for the officer's cook, he looked neat and was well perfumed. Everybody knew that the officer's cook did not perform any of the duties that ordinary soldiers had to. He did not even have to give the military salute, nor wear the beret; and instead of military boots, he wore sandals. All his work consisted of denouncing soldiers, and cooking food for the officer, and washing his clothes, even his underwear. The soldiers always avoided that kind of vile job.

I sat with the other soldiers around the dirty metal plate in order to have a loaf of bread, as I was doubtful about the cleanliness of whatever Hazem had cooked for us. The soup that he prepared for the nine soldiers lacked any flavor. He cooked one chicken for us, and reserved the other two for the lieutenant and the sergeant.

Despite all this, as soon as the cook placed the metal plate on the floor, the chicken was torn to pieces and disappeared from the dish, while the dirty fingers of the soldiers were swimming in the soup trying to dip the pieces of bread into it. The chicken's bones were falling from their mouths into the same plate of soup.

At that unpleasant moment I glanced at Sinan, beckoning him to snatch two loaves of bread, as he was closer to the plate. He actually handed the bread to me, and we were contemplating that nauseating scene. The soldiers were fighting to bury as much bread as they could into that soup, so much so that their dinner was over in a few minutes, and then they left, leaving behind the metal plate tossed upside down, and patches of soup and bread crumbs on the floor. Every soldier received six loaves of bread a day, and we carefully put them under our pillows while sleeping, for fear that some hunger-stricken soldier might steal them.

Sinan and I found everything at the battery unit strange. I told him it was important that we mingle with the soldiers and get them to tell us the secret behind such a strange environment. The opportunity came when the sergeant announced the night watch duties. My duty was two hours at the gate of the battery, from two to four after midnight. Sadeq, who was one of the soldiers at the battery, and a good person from what I could see, was standing guard with me that night.

I went to one of those mud-built rooms. It had no bed, and the floor consisted of pebbles and sand. Earlier, the sergeant had given me one blanket, which I had to wrap myself with to sleep. I used one end as mattress and the other as blanket. It was not really a sleep, but a struggle to get some rest before waking up for the night shift, in spite of the terrible smell that emanated from that blanket, which caused me to suffocate each time I pulled it toward my face.

I had only slept for a little while when I heard the voice of Sadeq saying, "Come on, we must take up the next shift now; otherwise we will be punished tomorrow."

I was so tired that I could barely stand up, but I urged myself up and went together with Sadeq toward the guards at the gate. They handed us the two Kalashnikovs. Each of them had only five bullets, which I found strange.

So I asked Sadeq, "The gun has only five bullets?"

I might as well have asked, "So, the sky has only one sun?"

He laughed and explained, "Don't be surprised by anything here. Just be patient and you'll see, hear and understand everything."

"Okay," I responded hesitantly before adding, "but I want you to help me understand what's going on here."

"I will help you," he assured me. "But do not expect me to answer all your questions."

It was clear that one day at that battery unit was not sufficient to build some trust with this soldier, who most of the time was alone, away from the other soldiers. After we had inspected the cannon, I asked him, "We brought food for thirty-three persons from the battalion, and I didn't see but nine of them. Where are the rest?"

"There are three soldiers in the secondary battery unit that is part of our own battery unit," he said by way of explanation, "and it's four kilometers away from here, and it has two cannons."

"9 + 3 = 12," I countered, "so where are the rest?"

"They're in deep sleep in their homes," came another cryptic reply.

I couldn't help but laugh. I said, "I thought that bribery was rampant in military training centers only; so has it reached the fighting units too?" He didn't answer me. So, I tried to ask him about something else, saying, "You ought to get those soldiers' share of the food."

"Hazem will be selling them tomorrow morning at the village marketplace, after which he will beg for alms."

"I don't understand what is going on, really. Do they sell the soldiers' food while they beg?"

"I'll explain what's going on here to you," said Sadeq. He proceeded, "Every morning, the lieutenant and the sergeant send the bread that they receive as food for the absent soldiers with Hazem the cook, who sells it to the villagers as fodder for their cattle. When he is finished with that, he starts his usual task of begging from the inhabitants of the neighboring village, and seeking their sympathy. Some people give him some money, others some milk or meat. His mental retardation and his shabby clothes aid him in carrying out this activity. His mental retardation helps him slightly too while begging, after the bread sale is over. Hazem then returns to the battery unit and hands over the proceeds, which include money, milk and meat, to the lieutenant and the sergeant."

Then Sadeq continued saying, "By the way, Hazem is not the only soldier who undertakes jobs outside the battery unit. Ammar and Hamza, they both work in the neighboring fields that are in need of labor, for which they receive daily salaries from their owners. In the evening, they hand their salaries over to the officer and the lieutenant."

"What forces them to do all this?" I asked.

"Nothing forces them. Hamza and Ammar come from the village next to our battery unit. They do this so that the officer will let them leave the battery for their homes, which are near, and spend the night there. As for Hazem, he is mentally ill, as I told you before, and he has no family or home. So, he tries everything he can so that the officers will let him stay and live at the battery unit. He has already completed his military service six months ago, and he hasn't asked for leave yet."

It appeared that the general mood at the battery unit was not a welcoming one to new soldiers. I was careful to avoid any problems, as I feared that any one of my actions could raise the suspicions of those around me, because the last thing I wanted was to be someone's enemy, especially since I was the brother of an executed man.

I asked Sadeq about the rest of the soldiers at the battery, saying, "Why didn't the other soldiers welcome me?"

"You must avoid dealing or mingling with them as far as possible. They're a bunch of thieves and drug addicts, so stay away from them. They're really bad, and they get the full support of the lieutenant and the sergeant."

"Who has the last word in this battery unit? Is it the sergeant and the lieutenant only?"

"No, the commander is Major Yasir, and he's on leave these days. You have to build a strong relationship with the lieutenant and the sergeant, because the major doesn't hold real power here. He has a weak character, and he fears the sergeant and the lieutenant."

"Unfortunately, I think the lieutenant can't stand me at all."

"He hates university graduates, because they dare to argue with him, and he can't easily rob them and make them pay bribes as do the other soldiers. This is why you should get close to Sergeant Abu Hisham. He is the boss around here in this unit, and everyone fears him. The young lieutenant fears Abu Hisham, because the latter is a member of the military structure of the Ba'ath party. The major, too, fears Abu Hisham, believing that he has supernatural and spiritual powers."

What Sadeq was telling me was extremely strange. I often doubted his words. While we were chatting, I heard some noises coming from the foot of the hill overlooking the river. I remained quiet for a moment, and then asked Sadeq, "Can you hear those sounds? They're coming from the river's direction."

"Stay here," he warned, "and leave them alone. They're soldiers from this battery unit."

"What are those soldiers doing by the riverside at this late hour in the night?"

"They're homosexuals," came his pat reply.

"Aren't they afraid that their homosexuality be known? Isn't this type of relationship unlawful in the army?"

"What are you talking about?" he scoffed openly. "There are five homosexuals in our unit."

"Do the lieutenant and the sergeant know about this?"

"Perhaps the officer is completely absorbed in intimacy with his personal cook right now," came his knowing response.

When Sadeq noticed signs of astonishment on my face, he said, "Don't be surprised. Here, drugs and homosexuality are indulged in without punishment, with the condition that they are done secretly." He then said, "Come on, let us hand the guns over to those coming to stand guard after us."

The days that followed were no different from my first day there. I had to go to the cannons of the battery unit and stay there until the officer pushed a button close to his bed, which set off the alarm announcing the end of the morning alert. The officer would stay in bed till noon, while his personal cook supervised the soldiers, and the officer would punish those who were not present during the alert after his midday breakfast.

The order for the morning alert came from the battalion. This meant that the Iraqi radars had spotted U.S. and British planes, which took off from the Incirlik Air Base southeast of Turkey, on their morning patrol to enforce the no-fly zone, which was north of Kirkuk.

In the early days, I was taken by surprise each time I discovered a new secret at the battery unit. Strange things were happening there, and the strangest of all was what took place during the midday heat, when the temperature was high and the shepherds were taking a nap. It was a funny thing, and a reprehensible one too.

Our battery unit was located on the bank of the river, in an area which is deemed a good pasture for the sheep of the shepherds living in the neighboring village. Since they were not allowed to come close to the battery unit, they had to take their animals to the other bank of the river for grazing.

As soon as the shepherds would fall asleep under the palm trees at midday, the lieutenant would order one of the soldiers to bring him a spyglass, which was of the "Tasco" brand. At first I thought that the lieutenant liked to contemplate the beautiful greenery around the battery unit. But he used to order the two soldiers Umar and Qasem, saying, "Come on, the shepherd's already asleep."

That was like a secret code, which, upon hearing it, the two soldiers rushed to the river, took off their clothes and jumped into the water swimming toward the other riverbank, and sneaked into the flock of sheep. I couldn't believe my eyes as I saw Umar and Qasem pounce on one lamb and carry it away with them to the river. They swam, each holding the lamb with one hand.

When they arrived at the riverbank that was closer to our battery unit, they plunged the lamb into the river several times, and then hid it among the reeds that grew in large numbers in the marshy land near the riverbank. The poor lamb could not move away; its wool was drenched with water, and its limbs were sinking into the mud, and the thick-growing reeds were like the green iron bars of a prison.

I used to ask myself: Why don't they hide the lamb in one of the rooms of the battery unit? Why do they leave it in the reeds? In fact, hours later, the vehicles of the shepherds arrived at the battery unit, and they asked the soldiers whether they had seen any of their lost sheep.

The soldiers told them to go to the officer, who readily answered them, "This is the battery unit right in front of you, and you can search it yourselves so you can be reassured."

The shepherds were completely certain that the soldiers of the battery unit were behind the disappearance or theft of their sheep, but they could do nothing. They would not dare to accuse any member of an army unit. Besides, even if there were evidence of the soldiers stealing sheep, no action would be taken to punish them. This was because the stealing was perpetrated with the complicity of the commander of the battalion, who shared the proceeds with the sergeant after the sheep were sold at the market in the city of Kirkuk.

The stealing was not limited to sheep. The soldiers conducted night raids in the fields of the village, stealing their watermelon harvests. But the villagers always found out that the stealing took place, because the road from the village to the battery unit was littered with peelings of melons that the hungry soldiers threw away, and which stopped at the river, where the military unit is located. What was happening was strange, and I always asked myself: Am I really in a military unit?

Our main tasks consisted of cleaning and maintaining the cannons, and of standing guard during the day and at night. The most tiresome of the tasks was standing at the second gate of the battery unit. One had to open the gate and close it many times because of the many visitors to the unit.

What was ridiculous about this was that the visitors were not members of the military who were coming to the battery unit to perform their duties, but inhabitants of the neighboring villages. They came there because it was the place where the most "blessed" man in Kirkuk lived, and that man was—amazingly—our own Abu Hisham, the sergeant of the battery unit.

Dozens of old women came to the sergeant's room in order to break magic spells, predict their future through astrology, or to cure their illnesses. The sergeant was shrewd and used unintelligible words, and was successful in extorting things from the ignorant villagers, like goats and sheep. In case the old women were not able to pay him with money, he would accept some meat, milk or dates.

It was striking to see that the sergeant's influence was not limited to ignorant people, but was strong even on Major Yasir, who would let those ludicrous things happen without objection.

Everybody feared the sergeant, especially the soldiers, who dared not lie to him about not doing their jobs properly because they thought he could read people's minds. As for the soldier Abdus Sattar, he was the sergeant's aid and participated in his "magic tricks." He was the only one who knew the secrets of the sergeant, and the latter used him to terrify Major Yasir and get the upper hand over him. For example, the sergeant would ask the soldier Abdus Sattar to throw pebbles on the roof of Major Yasir in the middle of the night, and make noises that would frighten him.

Abdus Sattar, who was a thin man, claimed that the sergeant hypnotized him and sent him to find the places where magic spells were buried, and he unearthed them. That way, he healed people who were ill, or made the spinsters get married, he claimed.

It was difficult for me to build any kind of relationship with the soldiers at the battery unit. To me, they were simply unscrupulous thieves. That was why I always avoided them as far as I could, so as not to get entangled in conflicts with them. But things did not go according to my wishes, and several times I had to confront them when they tried to humiliate Baha, whom I considered like my younger brother, and who still needed care and protection from that degenerate environment.

Most of the soldiers stuck close to the two soldiers, Qasem and Umar, as they were both on very good terms with the lieutenant and the sergeant, and they were their tools for stealing sheep and robbing the soldiers. The lieutenant used to order Umar and Qasem to steal the

The looting in Baghdad city was a very sad and disappointing scene. The American soldiers did nothing, beyond smiling and mocking looters, calling them names like "Ali Baba," while the excited cheers of the thieves reflected their understanding and interpretation of the "democracy" that had come to Iraq.

guns from the soldiers who slept during the time they were supposed to stand guard. Then the officer forced the soldiers to pay a sum of money, or face prosecution in a military court, with the charge of stealing state-owned weaponry, which is punishable by a prison term that could reach fifteen years. So, the soldiers yielded to him and paid the money, after which the officer returned their guns to them. This is also why the soldiers were at the service of Umar and Qasem, and stood guard in their place.

In this corrupt environment, I counted each and every day that passed by, looking forward to the day when I completed my military service. I felt lonely and secluded. Sinan had a peculiar way of getting away from this surrounding, as he could go home whenever he wanted.

The officer and the lieutenant were very afraid of him, thinking that he was from Tikrit, the birthplace of Saddam Hussein, which meant that he had relatives who held high positions in the military, because usually the high-ranking military leaders came from that city. They thought that he could possibly be a secret agent who has been planted amongst them by the military secret service in Baghdad, to gather information about the people in the battery unit. He was able to maintain that perception by his fair skin and the costly military uniforms that he wore; also, he could talk with a Tikriti accent, which makes the letter "y" sound like a "w."

This daily routine was interrupted by a national event. One day, the battery commanders gathered the soldiers in preparation for a referendum on the position of the president of the republic. Of course, there was no candidate for the presidency but Saddam Hussein himself, as if Iraq were incapable of giving birth to a leader other than that dictator.

We were taken in military vehicles to a military polling station. As we arrived there, the security officer ordered us to sing and shout, "Long live Saddam Hussein." He had a pin in his hand, which he then used to pierce the soldiers' fingers, and he ordered us to fingerprint with our blood, giving a "yes" vote to Saddam as president. We had no choice but to stamp our fingers next to "yes" because officers were placed close to the ballot boxes in order to supervise us, in case a soldier dared to vote "no."

The outcome of the referendum was predetermined to be in Saddam Hussein's favor.

4

The Executed Man's Brother

One morning, Major Yasir summoned me; by then my relationship with him had become stronger. He said to me, "Amer, go to the bridge near our battery unit and wait there. A military vehicle will arrive. Accompany whoever is inside that vehicle."

I was feeling resentment at the order. I asked him, "Why, sir? And where do I have to go with them?"

"I don't know," my commanding officer replied. "The battalion commander didn't inform me of anything. Go there and you will know why."

I felt that it had to do with my executed brother, but the battery commander preferred not to inform me of it himself. The tone of his voice and his compassionate looks increased that feeling that I had. He said, "Amer, control your feelings and god-willing, everything's going to be fine."

I could not but go to the bridge. It was close to our battery unit, about two kilometers away. It was only a quarter of an hour that I had been waiting, when I saw a military vehicle approaching the bridge and it stopped right before me. A man stepped out. He was wearing the dark military uniform with a red beret. With a harsh voice, he ordered me to get into the vehicle. Security officer Captain Falah was in the vehicle, too, which was driven by a soldier. We drove off toward the main street in Kirkuk. Despite my fear, I hesitatingly asked the security officer, "Where are we going, sir?"

His reply was curt and sobering: "General Ihsan Qasem has personally asked to see you."

The mere mention of his name—Ihsan Qasem—was enough to

terrify me. How could it not, as he was the commander of the battalion in charge of the security of the first corps, and also the leader of the fourth air defense sector, and was known as the fiercest person ever to have held that position. Many victims died as a result of the various torture techniques that he invented and put to use.

The vehicle brought us to the police station, where the office of General Ihsan Qasem was located. Captain Falah was uneasy and anxious. He said to one of the soldiers, "What kind of morning is this? Have I woken up early in order to meet General Ihsan Qasem?" While he was talking, the vehicle reached the building where the office of the general was located.

When we got out, Captain Falah took me aside and said in a whisper, "A report was sent from a Ba'ath party member who lives in the same area as you in Baghdad, and it says that you are the brother of an executed person, and you hid that information from us. Anyway, you are a decent and well-behaved young man, and I hope I can help you in this ordeal. Let me give you advice: keep calm when General Ihsan Qasem starts cursing and insulting your brother. Control yourself, because he will try to incite you by calling your executed brother all the meanest names." Then he added, "Tell him you're here only to serve your country, and that you do not sympathize with your brother at all."

I listened to Captain Falah's advice and remained silent all the way until we reached the office of General Ihsan Qasem. We waited for a few minutes at the door. Then Sergeant Yunus, the office secretary, came out and said to the captain, "Have you brought the soldier Amer?"

"Here he is," said Captain Falah, pointing toward me.

"You all stay here," said the secretary; "the general wants him in private." He then opened the door of the office, and I went in alone.

I introduced myself to the general, saying, "I am a commissioned soldier and my name is Amer. I am a soldier in the second battery unit of the air defense battalion."

General Ihsan Qasem, who was a huge and tall man, did not look at me. He was in his mid-fifties, and wore reading glasses. He was holding a file and browsing through the pages. I did not know what kind of documents they were. Then he addressed me, saying, "Are you Amer?"

"Yes, sir."

"What is your level of education?"

"I have graduated from the English department of the Faculty of Arts."

His reply was cryptic, but pointed: "The fault is not yours. It's the government's, which allows the children of the Shia to pursue their studies, so that they betray it later on." He then said, "Amer, you've committed an unforgivable crime. You've hidden information related to your treasonous brother from us." And he hurled all sorts of profanities at my executed brother.

I was trying hard to conceal all the resentment and anger that was in me. When the general found that his insults to my brother were not successful in inciting me, he began cursing me and my family. He came from behind his desk, and started beating me. I fell down on the floor, and he started kicking me, until he got tired and pulled me by my shirt, saying, "Do you think anyone can hide information from us?" He then yelled at his secretary, asking him to take me out of the office.

The secretary got in, blindfolded me and then I was pulled away by a group of guards out of the building. I think they brought me to another building. Then the guards took off the blindfold, and I found myself in front of another officer of a lower rank, who started to interrogate me. He asked me about my executed brother and his friends and what political organization was he part of, to which I answered that I knew nothing about that.

At that point he asked the guards to blindfold me once again. I was brought down a flight of stairs. I was deeply afraid. I don't know why I thought that they were bringing me to the execution room. That was possible, because at that time executing somebody would only require a piece of paper that was cold-bloodedly signed by a police officer. I was still feeling afraid when they took off the blindfold once again, and I found myself in a large hall, packed with inmates.

I immediately felt relieved as I got into that hall, because I found I was not alone and there were so many inmates around me. I asked myself why they had thrown me in prison in spite of the fact that I was a person who does not get involved in politics." I could not find an answer. I responded to it with perseverance, as I was not able to avoid it.

Every now and then I glanced at the door of the cell, hoping that the investigators would free me at any moment, after finding out that I was not part of any political organization. I said to myself that it was not a problem that I spent one night in prison, especially since my fear was diminishing and I had not been subjected to any torture. But that hope faded away as a group of prison guards opened the door of the cell; they were holding clubs. There was a momentary silence, then I heard the guards shouting these words: "To the corner, to the corner...."

I did not understand what they meant by their shouting. There was not enough time for me to think about its meaning, or to ask the inmates about that. They all rushed in horror to all four corners of the hall. They bumped into each other, trampling on those who had fallen down, and to my misfortune, I was among those who had fallen down. The horrified inmates' feet trod on my whole body, and I felt that I was going to die. But then I found that no one was around me.

The middle of the hall was deserted but for me. The next moment the guards were clubbing me all over my body. I was unable to do anything but look at them as they went for the most sensitive areas of my body and hit me there; eventually I fell unconscious. The last thing I remembered was the looks of the guards and their shouts: "To the corner, to the corner...."

I regained consciousness as one of the inmates was washing my face. One of them, whose name is Bahjat, said to me, "Why did you stay in the middle of the hall? You should've run to one of the corners, not among the first ones because you would feel suffocated as the inmates are pushing toward the corner, and not among the last ones as you will be exposed to the clubs of the prison guards."

Bahjat was apparently in his fifties, and signs of malnutrition were obvious on his face and his shaking hands. I asked him, "Why is all this happening?"

His response was blunt and sobering. "This is their daily entertainment. Get ready for tomorrow's party, as they'll be drinking a lot," he interjected with a smile.

I was hurt on my forehead, and I had injuries on my back, and the bruises all over my body looked like a colorful painting. I was actually injured more by the treading of the inmates running away toward the corner than by the guards hitting me. Days went by, and no one interrogated me. Although I hated their stupid questions during interrogation, I was so fed up with their "to the corner" game that I hoped they would interrogate me and release me from the prison.

Later I would learn why the wise men say, "Be careful what you wish for."

In spite of my efforts to get used to the conditions of the prison, it was impossible. The presence of Bahjat there helped me accept that reality. As the days went by, my relationship with him got stronger, while quite the contrary was happening between me and the rest of the other inmates, who always tried to avoid talking to me. Even worse, their looks were full of suspicion toward me, and I did not know why.

One day I asked Bahjat, "Why are the inmates so inconsiderate toward me, despite my efforts to get close to them?"

"This is quite natural when they deal with new inmates," he replied. "The old ones believe that the investigators plant their men among the inmates, and they convey whatever conversation takes place inside the cell to them."

What Bahjat was telling me about the inmates' concerns seemed logical. But his answer prompted me to ask him another question: "But why didn't you treat me like they did?"

"Well," he replied, "for two reasons. First, I have a long experience in this prison, and I am used to spies working for the prison administration being among inmates. And with time, I have become able to recognize them, even if they try to conceal their identity, which they succeed in doing with less experienced inmates.

"The second reason is that you've been subjected to violent beatings. It does happen that secret agents who are planted among us are subjected to beatings as an arrangement with the prison administration so as to appear as real inmates, but not to the extent that you've been subjected to."

As the days went by, Bahjat introduced me to some inmates, and they had deep trust in him, perhaps because he had been there in that cell longer than any one. The health conditions at the prison were very poor. There was only one doctor, whose only job was to confirm the death of an executed person after he had been shot, and sign his death certificate. Or, if necessary, he made up false documents to hide the real causes of the death of inmates who had been subjected to torture.

The great dilemma when one got ill inside the prison was whether to inform the prison guards that you were in need of medical examination. Unfortunately, I was caught in such a situation, when my stomach was aching. In the beginning, the guard showed great consideration toward me and asked one of his colleagues to take me to the consultation room. He appeared so humane that I trusted him, and he brought me into a room and told me, "Sit here, the doctor will see you immediately."

The room did not look like a clinic, but it was rather a large toilet room with nothing inside except for a chair stained with blood, which had turned black after it dried. Four prison guards entered, and started beating me with their wooden clubs, and tied me to the chair with a rope. One of them said contemptuously, "Do you know that stomach pain comes from the teeth?"

He pulled out a pair of pincers from his military pants, the kind that is used for pulling out nails, and they seized me and one of them pulled one of my molar teeth out. I was screaming in pain, and blood was flowing out of my mouth. He did not pull it out at once, but he moved it and then left it for a moment, and he did this several times. He then said, "You'll take a shower and everything's going to be fine."

They carried me while I was still strapped to that chair and brought me under a water pipe, which was high up. The water was dripping on my head, and they purposely did not open the tap to allow water to flow, instead they let it come down in drops. At first I was not paying attention to the water dripping on my head, as I was still feeling pain all over my body, beside the blood flowing from my mouth as a result of the pincers that were used to pull out my tooth. But after some time, I started to feel dizzy, which later on became unbearably painful. Each drop was like a hammer blow on my head.

I spent one whole day under the water pipe. I got back to the cell and did not feel any pain after that. The mere thought of these torture techniques made me forget my pains. A few months went by without my being interrogated by anyone. Like most inmates, I did not care to know about time. I am almost certain that the date, month or year meant nothing to them. There were no trials or interrogations. Once I asked Bahjat what date it was, and he answered me, "Don't ask about the date. You could be happy to know the number of days you've spent in prison if you knew that you were getting close to the day that you would be freed. As you don't know that yet, there's no use in knowing what date it is today, in order to avoid feeling depressed."

He then said, "It's enough for you to know that on April 28 you will have a sumptuous meal, as it's the birthday of Saddam Hussein."

My day at the prison started at five o'clock in the morning, with the shouts of the prison guards and their orders to us to line up at the door of the cell. We then got out and stood on an elevated pavement. One of the guards called our names, and woe to the one who did not say "Yes, sir" in a loud voice: the guards' clubs would be waiting for him. After that, we entered the cell in silence; we were not allowed to talk except by whispering.

It so happened that once an inmate talked loudly, and the result was collective punishment. They put the air heater inside the cell on, which they did not do during the coldest nights of winter, and the temperature started to rise inside the cell. We were in the month of June, which is one of the hottest months, and the temperature reached sixty degrees Celsius, which led to many of us falling unconscious. After that we were careful to whisper inside the prison, fearing the air heaters in summer.

As for the food, we had two meals of rice and lentil soup served in metal plates daily. At first I did not get enough, but with the passage of time I found myself rushing off among the inmates in order to snatch as much rice and soup as I could. Actually, I became an expert in racing to get food. That was the only way for me to get my food from the plate, else I would have to eat from what had fallen on the ground.

During all my incarceration at the military intelligence prison, I never took a bath. Bathing was a luxury in that prison, and there was not enough water for that kind of extravagance. Even if you had found water, you would not find a place to bathe in a cell packed with inmates. There was no space in its corner except for a plastic bucket that was used for urinating and defecating.

During my first days there the stench was unbearable, but with time, the olfactory receptors in my nose got used to it, especially since newly arrived inmates had to sleep in the corner where the bucket was placed. Sleeping further away from the bucket was a privilege restricted to those who had spent a long time inside a cell full of inmates. I had to wait for the transfer of an inmate, or his release, so that another one would take his sleeping place, and I would move to a place further away from the bucket by the distance of the man's height.

Many times I woke up in the middle of the night and found an inmate urinating or defecating in that bucket close to my head, trying not to make any noise. Since we were not allowed to stay awake after eight at night, the inmates tried to urinate or defecate without causing any noise, so as not to alert the guards. Many a time I was the cause for some inmate to be punished, as I was awakened by the drizzle of urine on my face and cried out in disgust. The result was that the guards would come and beat the inmate up, his only fault being that he was trying to urinate at night. The inmates preferred to urinate or defecate at night because they could not do these things during the day as they could not find anything to hide themselves with, and the night gave them some kind of cover, as the lights were turned off at eight o'clock at night.

Time passed by slowly. I had no distraction other than to think about everything during extended hours of absent-mindedness that would only be interrupted by shouts of "To the corner, to the corner...." Upon hearing that, I rushed off to the corner, but if I found myself in the forefront of the runners I slowed my pace so that other inmates would reach the corner before me, in order to avoid both the suffocation and the beatings of the guards. I became quite experienced in life at the prison, but I had to pay for that by many bruises and injuries on my body.

So, days were like one another in the prison, and, as Bahjat said, what was the use of us knowing the date if we did not know when the day would come that we would be freed? Of course, we knew when the twenty-eighth of April was, it being the birthday of Saddam Hussein. I would come to know another date, the twentieth day of October, 2002, which was when Saddam Hussein issued a decree in his capacity as the president of the council of the leadership of the revolution that pardoned all prisoners, civil and military. Although I was happy with that decree, I was anxious because the pardon was extended to those who had been convicted of theft and murder.

I was released from the military intelligence prison after four months and immediately rejoined the battery unit. Among the military prisoners that came back to the unit with me was a prisoner from Baghdad. His name was Hadi, who was accused of forging documents in order to get an early leave from military service.

When I returned to the battery, they were carrying out exercises involving "fire and move" maneuvers. The exercises involved firing on imaginary targets, upon receiving orders from the battalion. The soldiers acted as if they were loading the mortar into the cannon, and fired on imaginary targets. When the firing was over, they had to move the cannon and the ammunition in less than 45 minutes to another location 12 kilometers away.

It was a tiresome exercise, as we had to carry 50 crates with each of our six cannons. Then we had to dig the ground for the cannons and the ammunition, and pitch tents for the soldiers. Then we had to contact the battalion and inform them that the exercise was completed in less than 45 minutes. We dug by hand using shovels since the battery did not have any digging machines. The battery unit that failed to complete the exercise in less than 45 minutes was subjected to punishment by the battalion, which meant that all members of that battery unit including the commander, the officers and the soldiers would be deprived of leave for a period of 60 days. In addition, the food supply, which was not even sufficient to satisfy the soldiers' hunger to start with, would be further decreased.

The aim of these exercises was to prepare the battery units for a probable war against the U.S. The exercise was performed according to the time interval that the U.S. planes took to respond to Iraqi anti-air ground weapons—the air defense artillery and other weapons—and it was a time lapse of over 45 minutes, according to some generals in the Iraqi air defense.

In this scenario, the U.S. planes that we engaged by the Iraqi air defense artillery did not respond immediately. They returned to their base in Incirlik in Turkey, and other planes took off from the same base in order to strike the Iraqi positions, relying on the satellite pictures taken 30 minutes earlier. This meant that the time it took the U.S. planes to counterattack was more than 45 minutes, which was enough time for the air defense forces to move to another location.

The U.S. planes would strike the locations that the satellite pictures had indicated before, and which would be empty of any air defense forces. This scenario turned out to be real. We saw U.S. planes hitting places that were empty of any Iraqi air defense forces several times, as they were relying on pictures that had been taken 45 minutes before.

In the beginning, the officers took the exercises seriously. But after one of the battery units was punished, the exercises became more like a joke. After the officers received orders to begin the exercise, they did not do anything but wait for 35 minutes, i.e., until 10 minutes before the exercise was supposedly going to end. Then they lied to the battalion, saying that the battery unit had moved to a new location in 35 minutes, although they did not move at all, thus breaking the record and avoiding punishment.

The situation involving the UN and the U.S. on one side, and Iraq on the other, was close to explosion. The UN Security Council had voted in favor of Resolution 1441 on November 8, which allowed the return of the international weapons inspection team to Iraq in order to continue their search for weapons of mass destruction. That resolution was at the center of a row between the major countries, especially between France and the U.S., concerning their respective positions towards Iraq.

During that same period, the U.S. Congress passed a law in mid–October 2002 giving president George Bush full discretionary powers to deal with Iraq. As a result of all this, the military units were getting visits with unprecedented frequency to inspect their readiness for a possible war against the U.S. That was what led battalion commander Colonel Ahmad Shihab to pay a surprise visit to the battery, and he was the colonel who used to spend most of his time in his office at the battalion playing Playstation games. He did not know anything about the battery units and never went to meet the units.

The colonel arrived at the battery unit in a convoy of three vehicles, and immediately asked Major Yasir to gather the soldiers for inspection. As soon as they were gathered, the battalion commander started to show signs of annoyance on his face, and he turned to the battery commander, saying, "You are fit to be a shepherd, not a battery commander! Aren't you ashamed? What are these clothes that the soldiers are wearing?"

The Iraqi soldiers' clothes were generally worn and shabby. The soldiers in our battery unit wore shirts that belonged to one unit of the army, along with pants that belonged to another unit. As an example, Hazem used to wear the uniform of the armored units, while Sadeq would wear the Special Forces uniform, and so on with the rest of the soldiers.

The battery unit commander did not get angry over the criticisms

Iraqi cannons in the desert, surrounded by barbed wire, with an abandoned military police car behind them. Military police traveled in such cars, looking for and executing deserters or soldiers fleeing their posts.

of the battalion leader, perhaps because such humiliating remarks are common among the officers of all ranks. Then the colonel distributed new clothes to the soldiers, which had recently arrived to the battalion from the defense ministry storehouses as part of the plan to counter any possible U.S. attack. He ordered Major Yasir to oversee the organization and close examination of the soldiers. He also asked him to train the soldiers on using the artillery weapons. The subject of training soldiers on artillery weapons was surprising to all of us, since we had never fired even one mortar from our six cannons. Most of the artillery soldiers did not know how to operate a cannon. The only relationship between the cannons and us was that we would bring water from the river and wash the cannons in a casual way.

I expected war to break out soon. This expectation was further heightened by the U.S. media campaign launched against Saddam's regime, which itself was escalating its position and then making concessions out of fear of the U.S. bringing down the regime.

5

Radio Sawa

The next day Major Yasir woke up unusually early in the morning and asked us to gather. He informed us that high-ranking officers were going to visit the battery in order to inspect its fighting readiness, after which they would send a report about the extent of air defense's capability to counter any possible U.S. attack during the next four months. That report was also about the soldiers' training competence and the working condition of the Iraqi artillery. The battalion commander also asked him to train the soldiers on use of the cannons.

The air defense artillery was mostly of the 57 mm caliber, a type used, I think, by the axis forces in World War II. The battery unit did not have new artillery weapons. Most of its parts dated back to the seventies of the twentieth century, and you can imagine how suitable our cannons were!

The other thing was that the ammunition we were using was being stored in places that did not comply with any of the storing rules used in modern armies. Mortars that were manufactured in 1974 or earlier were stored in boxes made of clay. Do you remember that I was cleaning the ammunition together with some of my fellow soldiers? We were doing that using gas and pieces of cloth. I also noticed that some of the mortars that were manufactured in the year 1959 had the explosive materials coming out from cracks between the mortars and their casings, such that the head of the mortar, which ought to fit tightly with its casing, was so loose that it could be easily moved by hand.

The following days, the officer gathered the soldiers around the cannon in the morning and gave a lecture supposedly about how to operate it. In fact, all he did was to give a theoretical explanation about the 57 mm cannon and how it was capable of engaging targets as far as 5 km high, and about the type of ammunition, which was a cluster-bomb type that was launched from the cannon and reached the height mentioned and exploded with shrapnel, hitting the enemy planes. The officer did not explain how to operate the cannon except once, and during all these lectures we did not fire one mortar from our cannon.

Neither the battery unit, nor the battalion, was engaged in preparations for war. All the worry was about how to overcome the ordeal of the inspection of the battery units by the committee. This explained the preoccupation of both of the commanders of the battery unit and the battalion with the outward appearance of everything, from the battery units to the cannons to the soldiers. I did not see any real preparation for war.

The day that we feared arrived. A number of officers from the air defense command in Baghdad came to visit our battery unit and other units attached to the battalion.

The battalion commander accompanied some officers to visit our battery unit. Major Yasir ordered the soldiers of the battery unit to gather near the cannon. A few minutes later, Major Yasir, the commander and the other officers came to us. The committee started by asking about the soldiers and their health, and the food that was served to them, and their morale in the event of a war breaking out.

It was normal for the soldiers to praise the kind of food that they are given to eat, and their high morale, and their readiness to defend Iraq under the banner of Saddam Hussein. Everything was like a satirical scene in a comedy, acted out by soldiers to show their allegiance to the leadership, and their will to defend it to the last drop of blood. Of course, no one could say anything but that, or else he would find himself in one of those gloomy prisons.

After that, the officers of the committee asked the soldiers about the cannon. They were, of course, theoretical questions about the cannon and its operation and specifications. We answered most of the questions, as we had been given lessons by the officer, which we repeated over and over. We were like parrots. I am sure that some of the soldiers did not even know what they were saying, because most of them were illiterate.

It was funny to see the commander standing behind the officers of the committee and giving us the answers to their questions by making all sorts of hilarious movements. When the theoretical questions were over, the officers asked us to operate the cannon and load the munitions in it, and show how to target and fire imaginary objects.

When we mounted the cannon, none of us could execute what we were asked, and looked at the commander of the battalion, hoping he would help us by his movements behind the officers, but that did not happen. As the officers noticed that we did not know, they ordered us to come down. This was embarrassing to the commander of the battalion and the officers.

After a moment, one of the committee officers wanted to inspect the cannon to examine its readiness for war. He asked us to lower the barrel parallel to the ground. After we did that, he started to inspect it and saw some straw inside the barrel. He asked for a stick, which the soldier Sadeq fetched and gave to him. The officer put the stick inside the barrel and started to remove the straws. A bird suddenly flew away from inside the barrel. The officers of the committee were convinced that the cannon was not in good condition and reprimanded the battalion commander, then walked away in anger.

Later, I came to know that the battalion commander was able to avoid what the committee officers could have reported about him to the air defense command in Baghdad by paying a huge bribe to them. One could wonder about the source of the money that the commander possessed, and how he could pay such a large sum of money to the officers.

The answer is that the battalion commander was himself taking bribes from the officers of the battery units, in exchange for overlooking the officers who took bribes from the soldiers so they would be allowed to go home.

The commander's fear of the report was not because he was afraid to be punished and get his promotion delayed, but rather because he was afraid to be transferred to another unit in Baghdad, and that would mean losing his position as head of a battalion located far away from the inspection committees. There would be no opportunity for the commander to take bribes in Baghdad, as the units there are closely monitored, not giving him opportunities to take bribes, unlike in battery units such as ours.

Despite the unpleasant conditions in camp, I enjoyed a good relationship with Major Yasir. At first, our conversations were short, and were limited to his family and his only daughter, who was in the college of medicine. Most of the time he asked me to give my opinions about the problems faced by his daughter. He was interested to hear my opinion as I was a university student, and knew about the environment quite well; but he ignored my opinion completely as he had not studied at a civil university, but was a student at a military college.

After my release from prison, my relationship with him grew stronger and he felt at ease when he talked to me. I was, according to what he used to say, a trustworthy person. Maybe because I was the brother of an executed man, he felt comfortable confiding his thoughts to me, even though they were anti-government.

He often asked me to accompany him on his daily walk to a nearby place close to the battery unit, and he always stopped at the Sayyid Ali cemetery, which was an old one with graves dating back to the early twentieth century. Major Yasir used to pray one of the mandatory prayers there every day, perhaps fearing that he might be seen and then accused of belonging to an Islamic party.

In one such walk, and after the major had performed his prayer, I asked him, "Sir, you've never been a religious person praying regularly, but now I see you do that. Can I know why?"

"Amer," he confided, "I might die soon. The war is on our doorsteps, and the situation is getting more tense. It is getting to a no-return point between our government and the United States. Amer, I like talking to you, because you are able to discuss various things with me. I can't find one of those soldiers with whom I can talk. You're the only educated soldier, unlike the rest, who don't even know how to read or write."

"What about Sinan?" I asked him. "Why don't you bring him with you?

"I don't trust him, Amer. His look and appearance tells me he's not an ordinary soldier. He could be planted by the military secret service to send the news of what happens in the units to Baghdad."

Though I knew Sinan very well, as he was my friend since my days at the university, I denied having known him at all before my transfer to the battery unit. I thought that the vagueness surrounding him helped protect him from the officers' abuse of their authority over him, and the soldiers' harassment.

Instead I said to Major Yasir, "What made you believe that you can trust me?"

"I am not afraid of you," came his blunt reply. "Everyone knows you're the brother of an executed man. And this makes you trustworthy. I am almost certain that you hate the leadership and Saddam Hussein."

"No sir, I do not hate the president at all, and I pledge full allegiance to the party and the revolution."

"Stop talking like this, I know how much you hate him."

With the passage of time, I came to trust Major Yasir and feel at ease with him. One day he asked me about the radio stations that I listen to. I replied, "I listen to Radio Sawa." This is a station that broadcasts from the U.S., and it is totally anti–Saddam Hussein.

"Be careful that someone might discover that you listen to that enemy radio station," he warned. "You will get in very big trouble if they do." He then asked me, "Do you think the Americans are serious about toppling the regime this time?"

"Yes, sir. I think that George Bush Junior will fix his father's mistake this time, and the U.S. army will not betray us as it did in 1991, when after freeing Kuwait, it stopped and didn't proceed towards Baghdad."

He sighed in agreement and said, "I wish to see one of the U.S. Chinook helicopters land on this hill," and he pointed towards the hill on which our battery unit was located.

"Don't be surprised by my position," he warned. "This regime has worn me out and I have suffered a lot. I spent the years of my life in Saddam Hussein's ludicrous wars since the year 1986 till now. I took part in two wars, the first one against Iran and the second against the U.S. in 1991. Amer, the plight of the soldiers is much better than that of the officers. You're more like slaves for one year and a half. The officers are slaves for 25 years, and this is the time that I have to spend in the army, maybe even more. Do you know that, when I sign a soldier's military leave, I wish I could relinquish my military rank to his favor, in exchange for getting leave in his place?"

In the end of the month of November 2002 the international inspection team returned to Iraq, after a three-year break. But they too left Iraq after four months, on 18 March 2003, and I was convinced that the Iraqi regime was going down. The Arabic-speaking Radio Sawa and all the other western English-speaking radio stations were beginning to talk about the intention of the U.S. and Britain to go to war against Iraq.

At that same time, there was an international effort to draft a new resolution condemning Iraq. After several meetings of the UN Security Council, Resolution 1441 was passed on November 8, although France and Russia tried to prevent it. I was completely aware, just as all Iraqis were, that what these countries were trying to do was to protect their interests in Iraq. There was a rumor that was spreading among the Iraqis that Saddam Hussein had given away the oil fields of Majnoon to France in exchange for preventing the passage of a new resolution in the UN Security Council, and had granted contracts for huge electrical power projects in the city of Hulla, south of Baghdad, to Russia.

At that time, the soldiers could still take leave. Every time I went home on leave, I discussed with my elder sister the seriousness of any U.S. military action against Saddam Hussein, and whether that would be worthwhile. She was more doubtful than I about what could happen, as we were used to the hit and run tactics between the UN and Saddam.

Each time a UN resolution was passed, the regime rejected it in the beginning. Then, when it came under pressure, it would abide by it, and then violate it, and so on. We hoped that the international stance was not simply a media escalation. We hoped that an international resolution against Iraq would come out and not be implemented by the Iraqi regime, which would then lead to a military strike that would topple it. We knew well that war would cause the death of innocent victims among civilian population, and in the military, many of whom I considered to be innocent, too. I knew that as a member of the Iraqi military, I could die in this war, especially since I was in the air defense, which would be the first forces to be involved in fighting the U.S.

The U.S. was always successful in its wars because of its aerial superiority. That was in contrast to the poor performance and weaponry of the Iraqi air defense. In spite of all this, I wanted the war to break out that day, before the next. Millions of Iraqis were ready to accept a war that would last for several days and that would remove Saddam Hussein from power. He had executed many more Iraqis than a quick war could cause to die.

The vague Resolution 1441 was passed by the UN Security Council after some adjustments made by France. It did not specify what action to take against Iraq in case the latter did not cooperate with the international inspection team looking for weapons of mass destruction, indicating only that Iraq would face serious consequences.

On the sixteenth of March 2003, a week after the international inspection team had left Iraq, there was a meeting between U.S. president George Bush, British prime minister Tony Blair and Spanish prime minister José Aznar in a U.S. military base in the Azores Islands, and Bush talked about the time getting nearer for a final showdown with the Iraqi regime if it refused to comply with the demands of the international inspectors.

One day after that meeting, George Bush sent his famous warning to Saddam Hussein to leave the country with his two sons Qusay and Uday in twenty-four hours. I knew the war was inevitable, not only because of the news I heard on the radio but also because of the state of anticipation in the battery units of the 111th Air Defense Battalion. The preparation for war was fully underway.

The battalion distributed new blankets to the soldiers, and there was a noticeable increase in the amount and quality of food, which was expected. I heard from my elder brothers, who had taken part in the Iran-Iraq war, that the military command increased the food share of the soldiers before any attack. That was one of the ways the soldiers knew about any possible attack on their units. Also, the commander of the battalion requested the battery unit commanders to stop taking bribes for letting the soldiers go home, and asked them to verify whether the attendance of the soldiers was 100 percent.

The battalion also distributed protective masks against chemical attacks. There were courses on how to use these masks, and the serum to be used in the event of such attacks. The serum consisted of two tubes for self-injection. The soldier had to inject himself at intervals and attach the tubes to his shirt by means of a pin in the upper part of the serum container. The reason the soldier had to keep the tubes attached to his clothes was to let the medical team know the amount of serum taken by the soldier in case he was found unconscious.

It was clear that the military command in Baghdad was planning to use chemical weapons in that war, because the U.S. had never used those weapons during its past wars with Iraq. There were lectures given by Lieutenant Arif, the officer in charge of political orientation in the battalion, that were ridiculous and disgusting. They were all lies about the victories of the Iraqi army in its just wars, how the U.S. was defeated in the 1991 war, the perseverance of Iraq which came out victorious against 33 nations, the great evil that America stood for, the wisdom of the military leadership represented by Saddam Hussein, and its ability to bring Iraq to safety.

One day before the war started, the battalion commander, his assistant, the political orientation and military discipline officer in our battalion and the military discipline office of the first corps office ordered the soldiers to gather in the battery unit courtyard.

When we were outside our rooms standing in the courtyard, the discipline officer ordered the rooms where the soldiers slept to be searched. We were shocked to see them take the civilian clothes and the radio receivers of the soldiers and pile them up, drench them with fuel and set them on fire in front of us.

The battalion commander said, "We are soldiers in the Iraqi army, and we must be proud of the military uniforms that we wear."

Addressing the bonfire between us he said, "The only source for information about what happens on the battlefield is our leadership and our media. We believe this information to be true. And as we care for your morale, we have burnt these radio sets because there are enemy radio stations that seek to destroy your morale by hyping up any little victory that your enemy has, in addition to spreading rumors and misleading information."

In reality, though, the leadership ordered our radio receivers burnt to prevent our knowing the lies of the government media, and the extent of our defeat, and the places that the U.S. army had reached in its invasion of Iraq.

As for the civilian clothes, they burned them to prevent the Iraqi soldiers' deserting the battlefield. It was common practice for Iraqi soldiers to wear their civilian clothes under their uniforms, which they would strip off in the event of a war actually breaking out, together with their military IDs. This made it easy for them to escape the military discipline's monitoring, and also to avoid being killed or taken as prisoners of war by the U.S. forces. This had been common among the soldiers since the defeat of the Iraqi army in 1991 and its evacuation from Kuwait.

When the commander of the battalion had left, the political orientation officer gave a lecture about the wisdom of the leadership, and among the things that he said to us was, "You must never desert the battlefield. You must follow your brave officers and stay with them and fight."

At that time, the families of the city of Kirkuk were beginning to leave the city, especially those living near the air defense units, as they could be among the first units to come under U.S. attack. I watched the cars as they carried the belongings of the fleeing families. I felt a deep sorrow.

Although I did not feel afraid, I was sad, as I could die in that war and not witness the end of Saddam Hussein. I also felt compassion for myself and my fellow soldiers. I asking myself "why we had to expose our lives in stupid wars, and why we lived in fear while Saddam's sons enjoyed their lives.

All of Iraq's wars were ludicrous and not on an equal footing. The weapons of the air defense were primitive compared to the modern arsenal of the U.S. army. I wondered about the intelligence of our officers and commanders at that time, always busy meeting with Saddam Hussein, always telling him things that he liked to hear, such as that the Iraqi army was prepared to wage war under his "victorious banner."

I used to consider my fellow soldiers and myself as victims. We were only afraid that the coalition armies would not bring the Iraqi regime down. There was no way to get rid of Saddam Hussein other than war. I also feared that we would have to sacrifice the lives of many Iraqis as the necessary price for change. I thought I would be lucky if I could live to enjoy the post–Saddam Hussein Iraq, because the wealth that Iraq possesses, together with the intellectual minds of its sons, could turn it into the best and wealthiest nation in the region.

6

Red Flags

On the day that the U.S. attack on Iraq was launched, and hours before the ultimatum given by the United States to Saddam Hussein and his two sons expired, Major Yasir ordered the soldiers of the battery unit to gather. We all assembled in the training yard and, surprisingly enough, we saw both the commander's and the soldiers' cooks in full military uniform, contrary to their habit of wearing shirts and trousers without berets or black military boots.

The commander of the battalion came to us and said, "We're expecting the enemies to launch their attack tonight, at two hours after midnight. So, we're going to assign the combat duties to the soldiers of the battery unit and the cannons. We have six cannons, 33 soldiers and two officers: Lieutenant Qays and myself. We also have a warrant officer, Abu Hisham. So, we have 36 people. We're going to form 6 squads, each comprising 6 persons."

I watched from the corner of my eyes how the soldiers standing with me in the row were absolutely motionless and surprised, perhaps because they realized that the subject of war was taking a serious turn. Our days of squabbling over latrine duty had suddenly come to an end.

Not surprisingly, we were informed by the officer that there was a squad whose sole task was to punish soldiers who refrained from engaging the enemy by summary execution. He also told us that every fire team must set up red flags at the corners of a square on the ground, with the cannon placed in the middle.

The aim was firstly to determine the field of fire for each cannon, i.e., the area where the cannon was allowed to fire, and secondly to determine the area within which the soldiers were allowed to move.

Any soldier found outside that area would be accused of weakness and laziness and punished with summary execution.

Major Yasir was in fire team number one, and the lieutenant in fire team number two, and the warrant officer in squad number three. As for the rest of the squads, they were comprised of soldiers only. I was lucky to be in a fire team with no officer, because the officers would force the soldiers to engage U.S. planes, and that was something I did not want to happen at any time.

I was in fire team number five, which also included Sinan, Musa Manahi, Sabah Najat, Baha Tami, and Hadi. I trusted everyone in my group except Musa Manahi and Sabah Najat, whom I had not known previously.

Major Yasir ordered the distribution of Kalashnikov guns to each soldier, together with three magazines of ammo and two hand grenades. He also asked us to sign Document No. 106, called "the military responsibility document." It contained a list of all the equipment of each fire team, such as cannons, ammunition, guns, the radio communication set and a farm tractor that we used to tow the cannon and transport munitions after firing maneuvers. They distributed all that equipment to us on the day of the attack. The document indicated that anyone who did not live up to his military responsibility would be executed; e.g., in case any of the equipment was lost or stolen, or subjected to damage not resulting from air strikes during the battle.

Then he asked us to join our fire teams and take our defensive positions along the bank of the river, between the Tikrit checkpoint and the main road leading to the region of Huwayjah. Our maps showed a strip of land 30 kilometers long, along which we had to deploy our cannons.

The fire teams were 5 kilometers away from one another, and we had to carry out our combat maneuvers against the U.S. planes within that distance, which was short in military terms. The area that our battery unit was assigned to protect was the most likely one in Kirkuk to come under attack because of the military installations surrounding it.

To the west of that area was the Khalid camp, which was a large camp for the Republican Guards. To the north, Russian SAM missiles and the huge radar systems 67 (so named because they were old Russian radar systems, built in 1967) were deployed. The infantry had its installations to the south, on the other riverbank. The main road leading to Tikrit was located to the east and was a likely target because of its strategic importance in isolating the city. It was considered the second most important city, in the event of the fall of Baghdad, and it was also the birthplace of Saddam Hussein.

The fact that the military units were located along the riverbank was a clear sign that the military command wanted to provide the maximum number of forces in order to protect the northern front of Tikrit. The proof is that military forces were not deployed on the northern border of the city of Kirkuk, which was situated at the limits of the region under the Kurdish Peshmerga control.

We were to deploy along that same region in case the northern front across Turkey was opened. I was wishing that to happen, despite the Turkish parliament's refusal to allow U.S. forces to enter Iraq from Turkey, a decision made by the parliament on March 8, 2003, eleven days before the invasion of Iraq. On the map that Major Yasir had spread out on the ground, I saw our position among the other military units and I realized we were right in the middle of an area that was surely going to come under attack.

Major Yasir ordered the fire teams to start towing their cannons and choosing their deployment areas. The soldiers in my battery unit started to move their cannon and ammunition, in addition to the plentiful amount of food that the battalion had distributed to the battery unit, which was then distributed to the fire teams. The food included cooking oil, rice, lentils, broad beans and a kind of bread much despised among the soldiers.

The soldiers and I chose a muddy area at the foot of a small hill for digging holes, and left the cannon at the top of the hill for fear that it might get stuck in the mud while we towed it after having fired. We also dug a rectangular area, one and a half meters deep. We used wooden poles as a roof, placed sheet metal on top of them, and covered it all with soil. This, of course, would not protect us from direct missile hits, but it was a good protection against rain and shrapnel. We dug a hole for the cannon and placed our red flags around it. We also set up the radio close to the river and hid its antenna among the reeds.

We started digging in the morning and finished in the evening. I was sitting by the side of the river at sunset. The water was flowing quietly in front of me and I felt relaxed. I heard the sound of footsteps behind me. I turned back and saw Hadi and Sinan. I asked them to sit down with me, and said to them, "I would like to talk to you about an important thing. We must decide what position we must take regarding the things that are happening around us."

"What do you mean?" asked Hadi.

"We're only hours away from the war," I pointed out to them. "Any decision we make now will bring us to an end: either we save our lives or we die here."

They were very confused, and perhaps they did not understand what I meant. Maybe they thought I would ask them to run away. So Hadi said, "Sinan and I have thought about running away, and whenever we find it possible to do so we will."

I nodded. "That is a good way out and an escape from death," I said. "But until we find the right time to run away, we have to think of ways to stay alive. This war is not our war and we don't have to die for Saddam Hussein here, while he and his sons remain alive."

"Do you mean that we don't engage U.S. planes?" said Sinan, adding, "We could face execution because of that, especially since the firing squad will be supervising all the fire teams and will kill the soldiers who avoid targeting U.S. planes."

I shook my head vehemently. "I don't mean that we don't fire at all," I explained. "We won't fire directly at U.S. planes; instead we'll fire at another direction far away from them. The squad will only call us to account if they see us not engaging the U.S. planes, but they won't come and sit on our cannons to make sure we're aiming in the right direction. As we're a likely target for U.S. planes, the squad won't dare to get close to us. All they can do is count the number of mortars that we have fired after the raid is over. We have to always remember that the U.S. planes won't target us if we don't target them."

It was known among the air defense soldiers that U.S. planes targeted war matériel and not soldiers. So, if they wanted to destroy a piece of military equipment of the air defense, whether it was a missile or a cannon or radar, they would launch a missile at a location close to that equipment, wait for some time in order to allow the soldiers to move away from it, and then strike it without causing casualties among the Iraqi soldiers. That was almost like a war protocol agreed upon by the U.S. pilots and the Iraqi soldiers. Sinan and Hadi agreed with what I told them.

We still had to deal with Baha, Musa and Sabah Najat. As for Baha, he was so horrified that it was impossible to talk to him about what to do. All he cared was for us to stay alive. Musa was a problem. He came from a city in Tikrit and was from a family that benefited from Saddam Hussein's regime. He appeared to be very loyal to the regime.

Sabah Najat was a soldier who was suffering from a skin disease; he was allergic to the odor of soil, which caused him to suffocate, which

A crowd waiting to get into one of the Iraqi intelligence agencies' headquarters. In the turmoil following the invasion, many Iraqis tried to shed light on Iraq's troubled past by searching for evidence leading to the locations of mass graves of political prisoners.

was why we relieved him from digging in the ground. What was funny about Sabah Najat's situation was that he had been admitted to the allergy section of the military hospital of Kirkuk, and was called to duty by the battalion in order to reach its total mobilization capability. I wondered whether Sabah's absence would cause us to lose the war.

So, to keep those three away from the cannon, we chose Baha and Musa to carry the mortars, and assigned Sabah to operate the radio in order to keep him away from the cannon and save him from hard work. His task was to inform us that the battalion was calling our squad or giving us an order. Hadi's task was to fire, as he was the only one who knew how to use the cannon, since he used to fire when our battery unit was deployed to the north of Mosul, close to the no-fly zone limit.

As for me, my job was to aim the cannon.

The battalion sent us a coded message on the radio informing us that the alert level had been reached, which meant that we had to mount our cannon, load the ammunition, and stay alert, ready to execute any order coming from the battalion.

I was feeling happy, because the time for getting rid of Saddam was near. I also had a feeling of anxiety regarding my fate and that of my fellow soldiers and the Iraqis during that war. I hoped Saddam would be overthrown before I was in real danger, or was taken prisoner.

All this depended on what course the military operations would take, and whether Kirkuk would fall before Baghdad—or the other way round. That depended also on the extent of cooperation of the neighboring countries in allowing the U.S. military to use their territories.

I was sitting on the cannon, listening to the Arabic and English radio stations, as I had been able to hide that radio receiver from the military discipline committee the day they burned all the soldiers' radio receivers. All the stations were talking about the various possibilities, analyses and strategies related to that war.

Then I fell asleep, hoping to be awakened by the sounds of explosions.

7

Top Secret

The time was ten o'clock on a Thursday morning. It was March 20, 2003. I was listening to Radio Sawa when I was surprised to hear that the war had already begun. The news report said the U.S. forces had launched their first strike with 40 Tomahawk cruise missiles aimed squarely at a fortified bunker in Baghdad, where Saddam Hussein and his generals were having a meeting. I was disappointed, but I did not expect that a war the coalition forces had spent months preparing for would be simply a limited and unsuccessful missile attack.

I was hoping there would be a real military operation, one that would completely overthrow Saddam Hussein's regime. The feeling of animosity that I had was not only against Saddam's person, but against all the members of his repressive apparatus and the Ba'ath party as well. I knew that Saddam was not the only one responsible for the suffering of the Iraqi people, but all of his staff were and the Ba'athists who took part. That was why I feared that the U.S. plan would be to kill Saddam Hussein, and hand over power to one of the high-ranking officers. That way, we would have had a corrupt dictatorship replaced by just another military leader; one who would not be elected to power through ballot boxes.

On the morning of the U.S. invasion of Iraq, we received a number of documents in a file marked "Top Secret." These files contained instructions for deciphering the coded military messages sent through the Russian-made radio, which was manufactured in 1983. The coded messages contained complicated sets of numbers that had to be matched with Arabic letters. Only by decoding these messages would we learn the latest orders coming from the battalion, which could be to attack fighter planes or intercept cruise missiles—or even move positions.

It was foolishness on the part of the battalion to send us the instructions for deciphering the codes on the very day the war started. It was a very complicated code system and I do not think that any soldier knew how to use that list of symbols in order to decipher the code, as they were mostly illiterate. Hence, they could not take orders to fire at targets. Sinan and I found the coded messages difficult to decipher, as we had not received training on how to use them. But would we actually use the file containing the deciphering instructions? Two days had gone by before we actually did so.

The night of March 22, 2003, was a peaceful one, until late into the night. Then the silence was broken by the alarm siren of the Northern Gas Company. We then heard loud explosions, and a few minutes afterward we received a coded message from the battalion. It took me about twenty minutes to decipher it, during which time I could hear the roaring U.S. planes flying above us, probably having already destroyed their targets in the city of Kirkuk and making the message I was trying to decode all but irrelevant.

Even if we had deciphered the message in less time, we would not have been able to attack the U.S. planes at night. Firstly, I did not want to aim my cannon at them. And secondly, we did not have night vision goggles to help us locate our targets. When we could not see our targets at night, we would use the "firewall" technique. That simply meant aiming the cannon in a particular direction and elevation and firing heavily in that direction; creating a wall of fire in the night sky.

The soldiers of our fire team and I had pointed our cannon at a different direction from the one indicated by the information we were sent, and started firing. After the raid was over, we carried out the usual maneuver. We found it more practical to leave the cannon attached to the farm tractor, because to hoist the cannon with the hydraulic lift and attach it to the farm tractor would take some time, which we were badly in need of, so as to avoid U.S. air strikes launched using satellite pictures of the location from which we fired.

We moved to another position near the village cemetery. It was an excellent place to hide from U.S. aerial observation, and we were spared the effort of digging holes. The cemetery vaults were like rooms suitable for resting and sleeping for some hours, and were not places exposed to the firing squad's observation.

The problem we faced when firing was that the recoil of the barrel sent shrapnel in all directions, though fortunately we were protected by the steel armor plate of the cannon; otherwise we would have been hit by shrapnel. We also had to put up with the constant breakdown of the cannon, which Hadi repaired by the only means available: hitting on the release button with a sledgehammer. The cause of the breakdown was the old ammunition that we were using, which was unfit for firing.

We had received orders from the battalion that in case war broke out, we should use the ammunition that was manufactured before 1980, despite the fact that we had new ammunition manufactured in 2003. I asked Major Yasir about the origin of that ammunition and he told me it was Russian-made and was called "advanced ammunition," and reached a distance of 15 km, whereas the old ammunition could only reach 5.5 km.

I remember that he also said that the ammunition was smuggled from Russia to Iraq via one of the Gulf States, in ships made to appear like commercial ships transporting dates. All the time we were firing, there were vehicles driving at full speed on the main road all night long on the other side of the river.

The light of dawn was breaking. We saw military vehicles and ambulances moving along the main road behind the cannon. Inside those vehicles were the battery commander's assistant, Lieutenant Colonel Isam, a number of officers from our battery unit and members of the military police of the first corps. The vehicles were moving in a strange way. During the raid, they stopped from time to time, and watched us through a spyglass, and then moved to the other cannons doing the same thing.

We knew later that the people inside the vehicles were the firing squad, whose task was to execute the soldiers who moved away from "the battleground." This was a uniquely Iraqi military term designating a distance of 25 meters around the place where the actual fighting was going on. That area was delimited by the red flags I mentioned earlier, and it was the area we were allowed to move within, which only made a difference between dying at the hands of the firing squad or by a plane firing a missile at the cannon you were mounted on. The other task of the squad was to count the number of empty mortar shells to make sure we were actually attacking the enemy targets.

The U.S. air raids went on till the morning hours, and then stopped. The battalion did not radio us to inform us that the raid was over. We had already assigned everyone his duties, such that some would sleep while others would stay close to the cannon and the radio.

We did not do that because we wanted to attack U.S. planes, but out of fear of falling asleep and the firing squad finding that there were no soldiers near the cannon. In such an instance they would accuse us of laziness and we would be summarily executed. Even though we had assigned the duties in such a way that there would always be someone at the radio to receive orders and inform us, I preferred to stay close to the radio myself because I feared that the soldiers might fall asleep while on duty.

On one of the first days of the war, Major Yasir made a visit to our squad to inspect the cannon and the condition of the fire team. He was not wearing the military beret that he always wore. His clothes were spattered with mud everywhere. He inspected the fire team and the cannon, and asked us how we were doing. Then, as he was running his hand over the barrel, he said, "Does the cannon throw off shrapnel?"

"Yes, sir," I replied. "We could barely protect ourselves with the steel armor plate of the cannon, else we would've been killed by our own cannon." The major smiled. I asked him, "Sir, can the cannon work in spite of all the damage to it?"

"Yes, but it won't aim with precision. And the barrel could explode at you, because when you continue to fire with it, the iron ring around the barrel could blow away; that ring helps keep the barrel firm when the cannon is fired. Make sure you unfold the armor plate of the cannon when you fire; this will protect you from being hit with shrapnel."

The officer said, "Amer, you must always be mounted on the cannon as you receive orders from the battalion. The subject of the firing squad is serious, and attacking the U.S. planes is a matter of life and death for the military command in Baghdad. I know what you're thinking about and what you plan to do, but you must not rely on chance alone in order to stay alive."

During those difficult days I was only thinking about the moment that was passing by, and feeling that I was still alive at that moment as it went by. My thoughts never went further than that.

Even though the officer had already inspected the cannon and the fire team, he stayed with us until the vehicles of the squad arrived. I think he knew they were coming to inspect the fire team.

The security officer stepped out of the vehicle, as well as the political orientation officer and the battalion commander's assistant, Lieutenant Colonel Isam, who was known to be the highest-ranking officer of the military structure of the Ba'ath party in the battalion. There were also some elements of military police.

They came to us, and asked Major Yasir to gather the soldiers.

They counted how many we were to know whether any soldier had deserted the battlefield. It seemed that they were required to report the runaway soldier to the military secret service, which would inform the offices of the party in the region that the runaway soldier lived, so that the party would arrest and execute him.

The members of the squad began counting the empty shells of the mortars that were fired. A member of the military police turned to Lieutenant Colonel Isam and said, "Sir, they've fired 35 mortars."

"Good, good," said Lieutenant Colonel Isam, and added, "You are courageous men. I advise you to stay firm when confronting the enemy and do not refrain from fighting them. If we do not have victory today, then tomorrow we will. The enemy doesn't have the least chance of victory. We're the ones who possess all the elements of victory. Our leader Saddam Hussein, this historical hero, and your officers are most courageous. And we have a powerful and experienced army, and brave soldiers like you." He was talking to the soldiers without looking at me.

But when he had finished his speech, he turned to me saying, "How are you, Amer?" His looks did not show any real concern for me, or the ordeal that I went through the night before. It was as if his looks were saying, "We are watching you well, so be careful."

As soon as I said to him, "I'm OK," he put his hand on my shoulder and squeezed it tightly, saying, "We were there all night long and we know very well how you have bravely attacked the U.S. planes." He was pointing toward the other riverbank.

He said, "The outcome of the first day is: four U.S. fighter planes shot down, and 20 cruise missiles intercepted." I knew that everything this party officer was saying was an attempt to cover up the extent of destruction of the military sites in Kirkuk. It was a way to cover up the failure of the air defense to counter the U.S. aviation's strikes.

After a few minutes we received a message from the battalion informing us that there was a wave of cruise missiles launched against locations in Kirkuk. I could not believe the rapidness with which the officers and the members of the military police ran away, as if they forgot what they had just said about courage. The warning consisted of a number of coded messages containing a series of numbers. All the messages confirmed that Kirkuk was under missile attack.

The waves of attacks were so intense and numerous that we were unable to record the numbers of the code that the battalion had sent us, to inform us of every wave of missiles coming toward the city. The only thing we could understand from the warning messages was that cruise missiles were coming from direction 4 to direction 2, and that meant that missiles were coming from the north toward the south.

It was clear that the cruise missiles were going to hit either infantry positions or the city of Tikrit. We went to the cannon and, as usual, started firing at a particular point in the sky. It was a deafening morning, as tens of mortars were simultaneously launched toward a small area in the sky, in addition to the battery of type-56 missiles, which was located behind our battery unit, as well as all the air defense units firing 37 mm and 23 mm cannons.

We heard an explosion.

There was a sudden fire lighting up the sky.

One of the air defense units had shot down a cruise missile. I could not believe my eyes as I saw the missile falling and hitting the ground, exploding in an empty space on the other side of the river.

"Wow," Sinan said, "there will be a huge reward, at least one million dinars for each soldier of the battery unit." After the explosion we received a message that the raid had ended. In fact, we could hardly understand the message announcing the end of the raid, because of the cries of joy by the radio operators over the radio.

That happened despite strict orders from the fourth sector of the air defense, to which our battalion belonged, warning against talking on the radio device without using codes. But the soldiers, as well as the officers, were so happy that they forgot those orders, and each of them claimed that his cannon was the one that hit the cruise missile and shot it down.

They hoped to get the financial reward that Saddam Hussein and his military command had promised to air defense units that succeeded in destroying air targets. The reward was several million dinars for shooting down a U.S. plane and one million dinars for shooting down a U.S. missile.

While the radio was being used by the various units as a platform for claiming responsibility for shooting down the missile, a harsh and angry voice silenced everyone. The call was from the commander of security of the first corps, General Ihsan Qasem, who said, "Silence!"

There was a silence for a moment. Then the general said, "What is all this hysteria? Wait until we get the information."

We were all shocked to learn that the report was looking for the one who shot down the missile not to honor him, but to punish him. That was because the missile that was shot down came from one of the batteries of type-56 missiles, and had been to intercept a U.S. cruise

missile. But one of the units of our 111th Air Defense Battalion intercepted it and shot it down, thinking it was a U.S. missile.

Not one of those who were shouting at each other over the financial reward claimed responsibility for shooting down the missile, and
all those who claimed to have shot it down were now denying their
claims. A report from the fourth sector of the air defense put an end to
the disputes, putting the blame on the third battery, as the missile had
been moving within their field of fire.

We changed positions as usual. This time we moved to a location
far from our position in the cemetery. We also dug only one area for
the soldiers. It was senseless to spend hours digging holes in a place
that we would only be staying for one night. So, we dug only the place
where we would sleep, as our safety was all we cared about.

Despite the difficulties that I faced during the early days of the

In the first days after the fall of Baghdad, American soldiers were so relaxed that
they would walk around the streets of Baghdad without wearing a helmet. They
let the local kids wear their goggles and helmet, and the atmosphere was more
reminiscent of a visit by firemen to a local American elementary school than a
war zone.

war, good news was coming from the southern front. U.S. and British forces had crossed the Iraqi border. I was listening to Radio Sawa, and I was surprised to learn that there was stiff resistance in the harbor of Umm Qasr. In fact, I had not expected that those who suffered so much under Saddam Hussein's regime would put up such resistance.

I felt regret and sadness about the fact that our Iraqi forces were resisting in Umm Qasr, as they could be young soldiers who had been forced to fight, much as we had been forced. There was quite a difference, though. They were less fortunate than we were. Being in the air defense provided us with chances to save ourselves.

For the infantry, it was a different matter. Most of the time, they were groups of soldiers on foot who were hit by U.S. planes from a distance, and they were annihilated even before the U.S. Marines came within range of their machine guns or other light weapons. The battle was conclusive, and I don't think anybody had doubts as to the side that would raise the flag of victory.

8

Radio Communication Set

The U.S. air raids by B-52 bombers and cruise missiles lasted for several days. The grayish color of the planes and their seemingly slow flying speed were breathtaking. The B-52 bombers flew at very high altitudes, which made it impossible for our air defense to attack them. We could see our cannon's mortars explode at much lower altitudes than those of the planes, while the SAM missiles were diverted from their targets by the flares released by those planes.

The new location that our fire team had chosen was close to equipment radar that belonged to the battery unit of type-56 missiles. There were many mud-built halls belonging to this battery unit. The System 67 radar dated back to the Soviet era, and it was difficult to move it or carry out maneuvers with it. It was so huge that it took more than five hours of hard and continuous work to disassemble it.

One morning during the days of the war, while Hadi was preparing breakfast, and the rest of the soldiers and myself were around the cannon, we suddenly noticed a plane flying as if it were going to target a location in the area in which we had deployed our cannon. Usually, the B-52 planes would fly in a spiral before bombing their targets. When I saw this plane doing the same, I jumped off the cannon and shouted to the soldiers, "The plane's going to hit us or a place nearby."

Sinan did not believe me, until thick white smoke started to come out from behind the plane's wings, and the soldiers rushed toward the shelter. Strangely, each time we ran to the shelter during raids, we found it full of stray dogs, which seemed to have the same presentiment of danger we did.

All of the soldiers got in, except Sabah Najat, who refused to do so.

At first, I had no idea that his illness and respiratory problems were so serious that he was determined to stay outside that mud-built shelter, even though he was trembling with fear. So, Sinan and I dragged him inside despite his imploring us to leave him where he was, telling us that every time he smelled the odor of soil, he felt extreme suffocation.

The radar was hit by a missile launched from the U.S. plane. The loud explosion left the soldiers in a state of awe, and there was massive destruction around the place that was hit. I did not know whether to feel happy or sad about what I saw then. After the first missile had exploded, I was covered with dust as the mud walls of the shelter had collapsed.

At that moment Musa Manahi, who was known to always shout "long live Saddam Hussein" and was ready to fight the "American enemy," hid his head under the sponge mattress, as if that would protect him from the bombing, and screamed, "The attack's coming, it's coming, it's coming," and shook under the mattress.

In spite of all the fear in me, I could not keep myself from laughing when I saw expressions of horror on Musa's face. The explosion made a deafening noise, and the wind that it blew was violent. I was at the corner of the shelter while the other soldiers were in the middle. The plane launched another missile. Then it dropped a dark-colored object. It swung in the air, and burst into a fireball in the sky, and soon afterward that cluster bomb blasted the whole area where the radar had been.

Hadi was the first to see the cluster bomb falling down. He shouted, "Fire! Fire!" as he pointed toward the fireball. Despite the shock that followed the explosion of the cluster bomb, Sabah could no longer stay inside and jumped out. I watched him. He sat on the top of the shelter, near the door, pressing his hands against his ears with his head between his knees. I shouted to him to get in, but to no avail. He preferred to die by shrapnel from the bombs instead of dying from suffocation by the dust. As each explosion filled the air inside the hut with soot and sod, I wasn't sure if I could blame him.

The cluster bombs were exploding at a distance of less than one kilometer from us. We were eating breakfast, which Hadi had brought from the neighboring village, to which he continued to go while avoiding the surveillance of the security officers. Our food was all covered with dust from the bombing. Despite the fact that the bombing was intense and I was feeling extremely terrified I continued to eat, and noticed that Hadi had stopped eating, and was looking through an opening in the shelter.

I said to him, "Eat, eat; your mother has brought you to this world so that you would die on this damned day." I was talking to Hadi, but in fact I was talking to myself and blaming my mother for having given birth to me so that I would live that life which was, as far as I could tell, only perpetual horror. I felt that all I was going through was unjust to me. I was like a lamb feeding before being brought to the slaughter-house.

Our air defense sector had no ambulance to transport the wounded or dead soldiers after the air raid ended. The ambulances that were reserved for transporting the wounded men from the battlefield were used for accompanying the firing squads, in order to transport the bodies of soldiers who had deserted and whom the firing squads had found and executed. That was why I contacted the battery unit to inform them that the radar close to us had been destroyed and that there were many casualties, including deaths.

Major Yasir ordered me to take one soldier with me to carry the wounded soldiers, while the rest had to stay alert in case we had an air raid. Baha and I went to the military location that had been bombed, but we did not enter it as some soldiers told us that there were unexploded cluster bombs scattered everywhere. We were still at a distance from the radar that had come under attack and yet we saw many dead bodies of soldiers everywhere on the ground, burning and eviscerated. The melting pieces of metal from the radar were still on fire.

We heard the whining voice of a soldier behind the rubble of the radar. When we arrived close to him, only half of his body was visible, and we thought his hips and legs were buried under the debris. We were shocked as we pulled him and saw his body cut in half at his waist. I could see his red ribs from inside and parts of his intestines were hanging out of his abdomen. He was not alone.

There were a number of soldiers who were still alive, and they had been hit by shrapnel in the head, abdomen and other places on their bodies. They needed help, but we could do nothing because there was no engineer to clear the unexploded bombs and make a passage for the rescue teams. We contacted the air defense sector via the battalion, but unfortunately we waited for more than an hour while the wounded soldiers bled to death.

When the military engineers and the rescue teams arrived, most of the soldiers had already died. Baha Tami could not bear the sight of burning corpses and wounded soldiers bleeding, and he became hysterical and started to tremble. I pulled him from there and brought him to the fire team location. We covered him with all the blankets that we had so he would stop shaking.

I think that was the first time that Baha had seen dead bodies. He was extremely affected by that scene, which caused his already fragile psychological condition to worsen. He did not sleep the whole night and vomited a lot, and did not do any chores, as we had relieved him of his task of digging and carrying ammunition during firing maneuvers.

I switched on the radio, and there was a station broadcasting voice messages to the Iraqi army explaining the objectives of the military operations, which was not to hurt the Iraqi soldier, but to overthrow Saddam Hussein's regime.

It was also urging the members of the Iraqi army to stay away from their military equipment as they would be targeted by the coalition forces and destroyed. There were U.S. planes dropping thousands of pamphlets containing the same instructions. Even though these pamphlets landed close to our positions, none of the soldiers dared to pick one up, fearing that someone might see him and report him to the military secret service.

We continually moved positions, because of the many orders that we received to intercept U.S. planes, and of course we had to move to a new location after each firing maneuver. We were exhausted from digging and carrying the munitions all night long. In fact, after I had seen with my very own eyes what the U.S. planes had done to the radar site, I became anxious and wondered whether I had any chance of staying alive.

Although we aimed our mortars at the sky, and although we had seen the U.S. planes flying above our location, we were not in direct contact with those planes until the radar was hit. We felt the shadow of death getting closer to us each time we were forced to take a position that we had previously used for firing our mortars. That was because the strip of land along the river is narrow, and we could not move to new locations which the satellite did not take pictures of.

In addition to this, our battery unit was located in an area where other military units had been deployed, which made us easy targets for the U.S. planes. There were military units all around us, such that I could hear the soldiers of the infantry talking to each other. I think that that region, with all the teeming military units there, was more like a bowling game to the typical American pilot, since he was sure to hit a target wherever he launched his missile. It was stupid to gather all those units in such a small area; even I knew that.

I was sitting in the evening when to my astonishment, I suddenly heard Baha cursing Saddam Hussein and calling him names in a loud voice. I ran toward him and tried to muffle his mouth. To curse Saddam Hussein in a military site full of Ba'athist soldiers and officers amounted to nothing short of madness. Baha was hysterical and sweating a lot. I think that was the worst thing he could do while in such a bad psychological condition. So, when I felt that he was calming down, I lifted my hand off his mouth. He started crying in such a way that I felt sorry for him.

He was still a child in military uniform. I remember how he would follow the soldier with whom he stood guard wherever he would go, when we were in the battery unit, because he was afraid to stay alone in the dark.

Suddenly he stopped crying, and said, "I won't die here." Then he ran with all speed out of the area marked by the red flags toward the checkpoint of Tikrit. I think he was trying to reach the checkpoint to go by car to Baghdad from there. There was no time to think, and I called Sinan, "Sinan, let's get Baha back to the site, he's running away."

We ran as fast as we could in order to reach him. We feared that the firing squad might see him and kill him, or that some officer from the nearby military units might shoot him. Baha was running so fast that we lost any hope of ever getting close to him, and had he not stumbled and fallen on the ground, we would have never reached him.

We caught him and pulled him to our location near the cannon. He was shaking badly and raving. Sinan had to slap him several times before he came back to himself. Baha was not the only one thinking about running away from the trap that we were in. Both Sinan and Hadi had talked openly about that very subject to me.

Hadi said to me, "Amer, what else are we waiting for? The U.S. Army has reached al-Nasiriyyah and is on its way to Baghdad."

"Hadi, Saddam Hussein has tightened his control over the cities. So if we run away it would be impossible to enter any city without first going through the checkpoints set up by the Ba'athists around the cities. Take Tikrit, for example, no one can get in there without getting past the security checkpoint. Worse, we can't even move and get out of this area where we are without going through the checkpoint that the Ba'athists have set up in the neighboring village on the other river bank."

"We'll try to swim in the night along the river in order to bypass the checkpoints until we reach the main road that leads to al-Huwayjah," he suggested.

"As for me," I confessed, "I don't know how to swim. But even if I were among the best swimmers I would not take that risk because if I get caught by the Ba'athists, they won't just kill me but would go after my family and hurt them and you know why they do this. So, I prefer to die here or be lucky enough to be taken prisoner and stay alive."

"We'll run away at night. I'll talk to Baha about this after he calms down. He could come with us if he's still determined to run away, and he'll probably be safer with us."

I thought their escape plan was a good one, especially the part where they would take Baha with them. At night, before their escape, we agreed that we should keep the fact that they had run away secret from the battery unit as long as possible in order to give them time to get as far away from Kirkuk as they could.

We bade each other farewell, and they left, going toward the river while I kept following them with my eyes. I had a feeling of deep sadness. I wished they would not leave, because I did not want to die alone in that place far away from home. I do not know why I was always obsessed and anxious about my body's fate should I have died in that war, and about who would take the responsibility to bury me. I think that was why I wanted to stay together with them. I kept looking at them as they were leaving, and Musa told me, "Do not look too long at people departing; this brings bad luck because usually a prolonged look at the departing person is the last look."

I began to think about how to stay alive in an area that was under such constant, violent attack. The radio that was with me was a problem, as I had to execute the orders coming from the battalion to attack U.S. planes. I had no excuse to refrain from intercepting those planes when I received orders from the battalion through that radio set. Hence, I found it was necessary for me to get rid of that device in a way that would not let them suspect that it was done on purpose.

I had no other solution than to crush it with the wheels of the farm tractor while carrying out combat maneuvers at night. It would appear as though it were an accident during the fighting. I would not be held responsible by the battalion, and they would consider it as having been damaged during combat.

It seemed that the battalion tried to contact me several times, and when they found out that the radio was not receiving any messages they sent Major Yasir to inspect our fire team.

Major Yasir came and was surprised to find that Hadi, Baha and Sinan were not there. He asked about them and I told him that they had gone to the neighboring village to get some fuel for the tractor. The major said, "The battalion has sent me to check out if you're still alive."

I told him, "I'm sorry to have disturbed the battalion, sir. But, the device got damaged during the maneuvers and I couldn't inform you about that." Major Yasir did not show any response to the radio sets having been damaged, and I think he chose to overlook that. He only asked me to write a report about the damaged radio set so as to clear myself from any responsibility in case I received an order from the battalion during air raids and failed to execute it.

Major Yasir looked very tired and distressed. He said to me, "Amer, I think we'll be facing the worst things in this war because we are in the north of Iraq, and I fear that our region will be the last one to fall at the hands of the coalition. This will make us the last fortress that the Ba'athists will fiercely defend, and there would be a massacre should the coalition forces choose Tikrit to be the last city toward which they will advance."

He had ordered the rest of the soldiers to prepare the munitions for the battle so that he could talk to me alone, whispering in my ear. He did not stay for long, and went to his vehicle and started the engine. I thought he was about to leave, and I turned away and walked back to our location. He lowered the car window and said to me, "That was a smart move you made there," and took off to inspect the other fire teams.

Major Yasir had informed me that in my situation where I had no radio set to receive orders or warnings of imminent raids, I should rely on the alarm sirens of the oil refineries in Kirkuk, and the sound of other cannons that were engaging the U.S. planes. This helped me a lot as an excuse for not executing the orders of the battalion.

At that time, the families of the soldiers were coming to our units in the hope that the officers would sympathize with them and let their sons take a short leave. The officers refused to let the soldiers go home as they knew well that the soldiers would not come back to their units after their leave was over.

Despite the refusal of the officers, the families were often able to take their sons away home without the officers knowing about it. Sadly, this said as much about the ignorance of the officers as to the where-

In the days after the fall of Baghdad, young shepherds sometimes supplemented their meager income by selling cigarettes and whisky to American soldiers.

abouts of their soldiers in times of combat as it did about the stealth of the families in secreting away their sons.

The air strikes went on for days on end, during which we could not sleep. At least there came a day when a strong sandstorm gave us a little respite, as the U.S. raids on our positions stopped. I noticed that after that region had been subjected to cluster bomb attacks, the firing squads did not come to visit us daily, or observe us during the raids. Instead they came to check the cannon and the fire team at longer intervals and, of course, long after the raids were over.

9

Children Under Fire

In the evening of the day after my fellow soldiers had run away, Major Yasir came to our fire team and summoned me. I left the site hurriedly, and gave the military salute.

He said, "Stop this stupid thing. What military salute do the officers of the Iraqi army deserve? It's only a matter of days before our uniforms will be without any ranks whatsoever."

"Sir," I cautioned, "you seem not to be doing well."

"Amer, listen. We've got an order to move our battery unit to another location, but this isn't why I've come to you. I'm here to give you a three-day leave so that you can go to your family and let them feel reassured about your well being. I've got the permission of the battalion under the pretext that you'll be taking delivery of a new radio communication device as a replacement for the one that was damaged while you were on duty."

He was looking at me as if he would not see me anymore after that day, as if he was bidding me farewell. I saw tears in his eyes. He then said, "Come on, take your stuff and leave the fire team. No one knows what can happen the next moment. I don't want to say goodbye to you."

Then he turned and went toward the soldiers. I followed him. He said, "Are you still here? I told you to leave immediately."

"I'll bid the soldiers farewell and then I'll leave." Indeed, I bade the soldiers farewell, and when I approached him to say goodbye, Major Yasir turned his face away and raised his hand, beckoning me to go. But I gave the military salute to him, turned around and walked toward the main road leading to al-Huwayjah.

I was stopped at a checkpoint set up by the Ba'ath party. The guards were sitting on a wooden bench, while one of them—aged fourteen or fifteen and holding a Kalashnikov rifle—stopped the vehicles that were passing by, asking about their destinations and searching their vehicles.

One of the guards at the checkpoint asked me, "Where are you going?"

"To Baghdad," I replied. "I've been officially sent on a mission, and here's the order from the battalion to which I belong." I handed him the document, after which they allowed me to move through the checkpoint.

After much difficulty I managed to get a taxi to Baghdad. The 275 kilometer–long road from Kirkuk to Baghdad was teeming with military units along both sides. For the first time I saw Iraqi tanks deployed inside the neighborhoods of the small towns that we passed. There were checkpoints approximately every five kilometers, which delayed our trip to Baghdad, because we were asked to get out of the vehicle at each checkpoint, and the vehicles were searched and the passengers interrogated about their destinations.

I reached Baghdad at sunset. Everything in the city revealed that there was preparation for urban warfare. The pavement had been dug up in order to serve as positions for soldiers, Ba'ath party checkpoints and the Fedayeen. On my way home, some of my neighbors were looking suspiciously at me; maybe they were thinking that I had deserted the battlefield. Even my family did not come to me to welcome me and ask me how I was doing. My elder brother jumped to his feet and said to me, "What brought you here?"

"Don't worry, I'm not fleeing away from the war. I have been sent on a mission by the army. But, can't you wait until I get some rest after that journey, and then ask me questions?"

The situation in Baghdad was very different from Kirkuk. The whole city was mobilized, and one could feel the nervousness and expectation of the inhabitants. Everybody was busy buying food from the markets and storing it in their houses, and they also began to store water.

I noticed that winter blankets were spread out to fill the spaces between the doors and the thresholds, and there was adhesive tape all over the glass windowpanes. I asked my mother about the reason for spreading those blankets in that way on the doorsteps.

She answered me saying, "My dear boy, your brother Majid thinks that Saddam Hussein will fight in order to stay alive and remain in power. So, if the Americans occupy Baghdad, he could resort to attacking the city with chemical weapons, just as he did with the Kurdish cities with those weapons that are in his possession. That is why we keep these blankets close to the openings at the thresholds, so that in case we are attacked with chemical weapons we'll dampen them with water."

The U.S. strikes against the military positions close to our house were not the only things that preoccupied my mother. The presence of air defense units in the neighborhoods was a source of great danger as they were targeted by U.S. planes. There were also civilian casualties from falling mortars and missiles of the air defense.

These were supposed to explode in the air far from the houses. Perhaps my relatives did not know why the mortars and missiles launched by the air defense units were falling back, but I knew it was because they were old and unfit for use in combat. On my first day in Baghdad I saw mortars falling on civilian houses, resulting in casualties. I wondered where the mortars that we had fired from our cannons had fallen.

We constantly listened to the news. Twelve days had elapsed since the U.S. invasion, and the city of Najaf was under siege. In the city of Karbala, fierce fighting was going on between units of the Iraqi army and the U.S. forces.

Of course, my relatives asked me how I was doing. I told them that I was doing very well, and that my unit had not yet taken part in any battle, and had not been subjected to air strikes, and that we were in a much better condition than the civilians in Baghdad. I told them that in Kirkuk we were not fighting, but just waiting for Baghdad to fall so that we could get back there.

My first night of leave in Baghdad was a real horror. Tons and tons of bombs were falling everywhere. The area where I lived was under heavy bombing, as it was close to Saddam International Airport and the Presidential Palace in al-Radwaniyah, which was the residence of the younger wife of Saddam Hussein. It was devastating to see my nephew trembling with fear, so I held him in my arms and said to him, "Don't be afraid, dear. I'm your uncle and I'll be afraid in your place. You need not be afraid, okay?"

My mother used to gather all the children of the family in a small room which served as a store, after she had emptied it and made it a shelter. I do not know what was special about that particular room, nor what made it safer than the other ones.

During raids, my mother would gather the children in that room, and would get completely absorbed in prayer and supplication, which she said loudly as though she was trying to keep the danger away with the volume of her prayers. And each time she heard a bomb hit its target on the ground and explode, she would scream; trying to make her voice louder than the explosion so that the children would not be afraid.

The adults in our house refused to go to the small store room despite my mother's urging them to do so, but I went to the store room and put my head in her lap, and pressed both her hands on my ears so that I would not hear the sounds of explosion, and then I cried. I wiped my tears before they fell in her lap so that she would not know I was weeping. Fortunately, my mother was so absorbed in her prayers to God that she did not notice me crying.

In the morning, I decided to go out of my house for some time. I was stopped by Abu Zeena in the street. He was a Ba'ath party member in our area. He asked me a question, which he tried to put to me jokingly: "You've run away from the army?"

I replied, trying to throw away that accusation which could lead to death, "No. I'm on a military assignment," and presented the letter of the assignment which the battalion had given me to him. He took the letter to check whether I was telling the truth, and then gave it back to me saying, "I know you're a brave man. I just wanted to feel reassured about you, because I have deep respect and love for your family."

His lie was obvious, and we were almost certain that he was the Ba'ath party member who had reported my executed brother Ahmed. I left him and went to pay a visit to one of my friends in the area where I lived. His name was Tahseen, and his father was a member of the Ba'ath party. Tahseen was also a member of the Ba'ath party's student organization in college. He was carrying out his guard duty and night watch in his residential area.

I went to his house in the hope of meeting him, and was informed by his mother that he was in a detachment of the Ba'ath party. I went to the office of the party and there I saw him sitting among fat-bellied members of the Arab Socialist Ba'ath Party. Their military uniforms, their behavior, and the way they dealt with people made them look like fierce fighters. But their huge bellies and hind ends made them look quite the contrary. I wondered whether those elephants would ever be able to use hit-and-run tactics and move quickly through the alleys of Baghdad in case there was urban warfare.

As soon as Tahseen saw me, he stood up from among them and looked down as if he were ashamed that I had seen him sitting with those people. He asked permission from his party superior and came toward me.

I told him, "Let's go somewhere else; I want to talk to you in private."

"Okay," replied Tahseen.

I said to him, "Are you crazy? You've got yourself into this thing. Haven't I told you not to attend the meetings of the party? Look what you've got yourself into now. You will have to defend Baghdad until you die."

"It isn't me who's crazy, it's you. Lower your voice, else we're both going to pay the price of your reckless behavior. Listen, the Americans aren't going to reach Baghdad."

He said that in a confident voice, as if he seriously believed it. Then he told me that the party leadership had armed all the students, and that the war would turn into urban warfare, and that we would be victorious.

"America does not want to get into urban warfare, because it is afraid that the casualties among its soldiers might be high, which is why it will rely on air strikes and not enter the cities. Don't you see that they've not entered any Iraqi city?" he asked.

I interrupted him, saying, "They will enter Baghdad and it's going to be a fierce battle if the Ba'athists try to desperately defend the city, although I doubt whether they'll fight."

"I've taken a short leave from the comrades," he told me, as if he wanted to end his conversation with me. He added, "Amer, if I stay at the party's office in our area during the war, I won't be considered failed this year. The university has told us so."

"I hope you'll remain alive in order that you might get this reward."

"Don't take things too seriously. We stand guard until one o'clock at night, then the students of the secondary schools stand guard after us."

I laughed at him and said, "I've got to go now."

The airport and its surrounding area were under heavy bombing. It was obvious that the coalition forces were pressing toward Baghdad. The units of the Republican Guards were deployed in the residential areas, and the soldiers had taken their positions in the secondary roads.

Despite being a realistic person, I could not imagine the extent of damage that would be inflicted on my city if it were caught in a crossfire between the Republican Guards and the Marines advancing toward it. At that time, there was a most disturbing statement put out by a

Scenes of the countryside along the route I took when escaping from Kirkuk to Baghdad.

high-level Iraqi official, the minister of defense Hashim Sultan, which surprised me. He said, "The enemy forces will reach Baghdad in five to ten days."

On the morning of the second day of my leave in Baghdad, I had to wear civilian clothes and go to a house in the eastern Karadah neighborhood. It was a reserve workshop for repairing radio communication devices for the ministry of defense. The workshop was a somewhat isolated house located in a residential area and was used as a disguise in order to avoid air strikes, a method widely used to protect military sites.

Such units were moved to houses in the middle of residential areas and the people working there—as well as those coming to visit—were asked to wear civilian clothes. This preventive measure was not enough, though, to protect the disguised units. Quite the contrary; they were bombed, however hidden in the residential areas they happened to be, as U.S. intelligence was aware of what was going on in Baghdad through its agents. It was sad that those units caused the destruction of the houses close to them when they were bombed by U.S. planes.

There were no new communication sets at the workshop. I met the workshop manager and asked him to provide our battery unit with one. He said, "How can I give you a new radio set? There are no more communication devices left in the storehouse. After all, I can't understand why it's always the radio communication devices that are the first things to get destroyed in the war." I left the workshop manager feeling happy not to get a new radio set; otherwise I would have had to find another way to destroy it.

My elder brother advised me not to return to the battery unit, and instead to stay home and hide until the fall of Baghdad. I was in a very difficult dilemma, because if I deserted the military and was arrested later on, I would end up being executed. But if I joined the military again, I would face death too. I was sitting in the living room when my elder brother came in. He sat close to me, and said, "Amer, what's your decision? You will return or not?"

I replied, "I don't know. Tell me what you think." I was throwing the ball in his court, and hoped at that moment that he would say to me, "Don't go; stay here," as my other brother had told me.

But my elder brother said, "Amer, our lives are in God's hands; you could be saved and return back safely. Believe me, no one knows the intentions of Saddam or the coalition forces. Nobody can understand politics because it's dirty and it breaks its promises. We don't know what could happen to you if you desert and Saddam stays in power and the coalition forces do not overthrow him. They will surely come and break into your house and humiliate everybody. Who knows what could happen after that? They'll execute you as they did your brother."

I nodded and said to him, "God willing, I will make my decision tomorrow."

I tried to sleep, but in vain. In the middle of the night I made up my mind to return to the battery unit. I put my clothes in my bag and shaved. After everything was ready, I woke up my mother and said goodbye to her. I was determined to leave for the front at night, because I feared I might change my decision if I woke up in the morning and someone in my family persuaded me to stay.

10

It Is All Over

I arrived in Kirkuk and went to the location of the fire team. I was expecting that it would not be where I left it, because it had to change positions as a result of engaging U.S. planes. I was thinking that the fire team's location could not be far from the riverside, which was where it had to carry out its combat duties. However, I did not find the fire team, so I went to fire team number one, which was under the supervision of Major Yasir. I was surprised to find that all the fire teams were assembled there.

The soldiers were surprised that I had returned back, maybe because they thought that I would never come back. I went toward Major Yasir. He was listening to the radio. I said, "How are you, sir?"

He turned to me and replied. "I was hoping that you would not come back, but I knew you would." He laughed and said to me, "What are you doing here? U.S. forces have been airdropped onto the airport in Baghdad—and you're here?"

I was stunned by that news, as I could not imagine this happening. The day before I had been in Baghdad and I had not heard anything about that. Could it be that they had reached Baghdad so rapidly?

I asked Major Yasir, "Is this why you've gathered all the fire teams in one place?"

"No," he explained, "we got an order from the commander of the fourth sector of the air defense to do so, and I don't know why. Maybe the commander wants to strengthen the air defense around this main road, which links Tikrit with Kirkuk. As you know, this road is of strategic importance for whoever wants to win the final battle."

"Baghdad is supposed to be the decisive battle," I countered, "and not Tikrit."

"I don't think so, because troops are massing around Tikrit, and all the orders that we receive are coming from Tikrit and not Baghdad. This means that the army command is now based in Tikrit."

The massing of troops became more intense near the Tikrit-Kirkuk main road. The Republican Guards and the infantry units had dug the whole area along that road, which looked like rabbit holes, and one had to be careful while walking there in order to avoid falling into one of them.

I asked Major Yasir for permission to go to my fire team's location. To my astonishment, I saw Baha, Sinan and Hadi near the cannon. I had mixed feelings of happiness and surprise. I said to them, "Why are you here?"

"We have miraculously escaped from the Fedayeen forces," replied Sinan.

"Were you caught by them?"

"No, thank God. We ran away from them. If they had caught us, they would've arrested us and sent us to the front in al-Hillah to fight."

At that time, the Ba'athists and the Fedayeen were forcing the soldiers who were fleeing the city of Kirkuk to go fight in the southern cities. They arrested them and brought them to the battlegrounds in those cities, and the soldiers who refused to comply were summarily executed.

I said to Sinan, "Praise God that you're safe and sound. I'm happy you're back, because I'm sure now there will be someone here to take charge of my burial should I be killed." I was feeling uneasy about us having been moved and assembled close to the officers, as it meant that they would force us to engage the U.S. planes.

A long time went by when I did not meet Lieutenant Qays nor warrant officer Abu Hisham and the soldiers of the battery unit. We were on different fire teams. Everybody was anxious about the news that U.S. forces had been airdropped onto Saddam Airport, except for me. I saw that the occupation of the airport was a foothold that the coalition forces had gained inside Baghdad, from where they could advance and take over the city completely. I used to ask Major Yasir permission to go to the river with my radio hidden under my clothes. There were contradicting reports.

The Iraqi minister of information, Muhammad Saeed al-Sahhaf, was speaking in a way that showed he was completely confident about what he was saying. His declarations were a series of lies about U.S. tanks burning and high casualties among U.S. soldiers. Al-Sahhaf's words were oft-repeated and meaningless clichés, such as: "Great victory; the enemy's heavy losses; crushing counter-attack against the enemy."

My ears were used to hearing those words ever since the days of the Iran-Iraq war until the battles of these days. I did not care about what al-Sahhaf was saying. I was taking all my information about what was going on from the "enemy's media outlets," as they were described by Iraqi military intelligence.

All that worried me about the U.S. army's control over the airport was the extent of damage to the surrounding areas. My family lived at a distance of less than two miles from the northeast of the airport, and for any ground combat to seize control of it the surrounding areas would have to be heavily bombed in addition to suffering battles involving tanks. I could not imagine the convoys of tanks moving through residential areas.

I was certain that the Republican Guard forces I saw in the area where I lived would give away the airport easily, and I knew that the Saddam Airport was the key for getting control over the capital, as it could be used for airdrops of U.S. forces and supplies. And if that battle were lost, the coalition forces would have to rely on long transport routes which extend from Kuwait to Baghdad on roads where the Republican Guards had set ambushes, which would delay the advance of the coalition towards Baghdad. The U.S. military command would be concerned about the advance of its forces toward Baghdad and the protection of those forces against such ambushes, since the Republican Guards had been well trained for this kind of warfare.

The U.S. air raids on our positions in Kirkuk continued, especially on the positions near the river. We were in the middle of thousands of soldiers of the Republican Guards and the infantry who had taken position close to the main road linking Tikrit to Kirkuk. We were exposed just like them to the danger of the continuous raids. At midday Major Yasir was informed of a possible U.S. raid on our position.

We went to the cannons, and in less than ten minutes U.S. fighter planes were flying above us. We could not fire until we received the order from the officers, as these were the new firing instructions that warrant officer Abu Hisham informed us of. The planes continued to fly above us, but the firing order was not given yet. When it finally came, I did not hear the officer giving the order. It was simply a gunshot, which I heard mixed with the sounds of roaring planes in the cloudy sky. The cannons of the other fire teams began to fire, except ours. Hadi shouted,

"Fire far away from the planes, the major has fired his gun!" That shot was the order to fire.

As usual, I started aiming my cannon's mortars away from the raiding U.S. planes. They were flying at low altitudes and performing rapid climbing and diving maneuvers; then they disappeared in the clouds, together with the roaring sounds. Suddenly they appeared from another direction and fired their missiles at the positions of the Republican Guards around us. It was a terrifying scene.

I could feel the blowing air from the exploding missiles pressuring all my body, and I felt that I was being lifted up from the cannon and hurled a distance away from it. There were screams everywhere around me and all I could hear was a continuous ringing sound.

The sky turned into mere dust and smoke. I ran toward a deep hole, stumbling over torn off bodies of the soldiers, to take refuge against the missiles raining down. I did not notice that the foolish military command had placed dummy plastic missiles as camouflage and for using up U.S. ammunition.

I could not have imagined such military foolishness in a war of that magnitude; using plastic missiles in order to draw the attention of the U.S. aviation so they would target them, but placed in the middle of Iraqi forces. I changed my mind, and instead of going to a deep hole, I lay flat on the ground, and I saw the U.S. planes hitting the plastic missiles close to the shelter, which caused the soldiers inside to be buried alive. The raid did not last long. When it ended, there came out of the reeds growing on the riverbank our "brave officers."

Their clothes were covered with mud. Their faces were covered with dirt, too. I could not imagine that "our brave officers" would hide among the reeds on the river bank and give us orders to fire from there by means of shooting with their guns, while death was getting close to me and whispering in my ears.

As usual, we evacuated the dead bodies using the farm tractors. The victims' corpses were carried and transported as if they were slaughtered sheep, because the officers would not allow that their own military vehicles be used, lest they were spattered with blood. The corpses were driven to the military hospital of Kirkuk. And if anyone wanted to know where the hospital was, he just had to follow the trails of blood that the farm tractor left behind.

I think we were fooling ourselves by changing positions within a perimeter of less than five kilometers, which was the area that we were allowed to move within according to the plan drawn by the ingenious air defense command. I think that the safety of the soldiers massing in an area of less than five kilometers was less of a priority than massing soldiers according to tactics used in the middle ages, which was the only thing that mattered.

It was the fourth of April, and sixteen days had elapsed since the war started. That day witnessed the capture of Saddam International Airport by U.S. forces. News came in about the capture of the airport and that it was renamed "Baghdad International Airport" as before. There were undoubtedly fierce battles inside and around the airport, and I am sure these were the fiercest during the war. The U.S. forces' control over the airport meant that they were twenty minutes away from the center of Baghdad, by the Hummer military vehicles.

The airport was linked by a highway from its northeastern side to the outskirts of the city and to the city center. Of course, the Iraqi command did not acknowledge the capture of the airport and insisted that it still had "complete control" of it, and that the U.S. forces had been "driven out of it."

In spite of the fact that I was a strong supporter of U.S. military intervention to drive Saddam Hussein out of power, I began to worry about the fate of my family. Our living conditions as soldiers were getting worse. Our stock of food was used up. Food supplies from the battalion had been cut off as the storehouses of the air defense sector had been hit. We had to buy our food from the neighboring village, where the traders were exploiting our need for food by raising prices, using the scarcity of food as a pretext.

It was as if we were not an army of that nation, because if we were really its protectors it would not have dealt with us on the basis of profit or loss. The inhabitants of that village were Kurds whose fertile lands had been snatched away from them under many pretexts, and annexed to the farms of the vice-president of the republic, Izzat Ibrahim al-Douri.

The inhabitants of that village had every right to treat the soldiers of the Iraqi army in that manner, since they had suffered many injustices at the hands of that army in the eighties of the twentieth century and before that until the year 1991, just because they were Kurds. Their bitter experiences with those wearing the khaki uniforms were well known: destruction of towns, bombing of villages and random executions, just because they were from a different ethnic group than those in power.

They considered all the Iraqi soldiers criminals, even those who had not done anything to them. I will not forget the time we had to go through a village while carrying out a maneuver. The children were playing in the lanes of the village, rejoicing innocently, and as they saw us entering the village with our cannons, they ran screaming in fear. They were stammering Kurdish words, and although I did not understand I was sure those words meant "the murderers are here."

Moments later, the old women were standing at the doors of their houses shouting "long live Saddam Hussein" and praising the great achievements made by the Arab Socialist Ba'ath Party, in broken Arabic and pronouncing the Arabic letters in a funny way. We did not see any of the men of the village. They were surely hiding inside their homes out of fear of our presence. Perhaps they thought we were an artillery battalion about to destroy their village once more.

There were fears that the Kurdish inhabitants would carry out retaliatory attacks against the Iraqi soldiers in revenge for the repression and persecution that they had suffered at the hands of the central government in Baghdad. I was not afraid of that, as Sabah Najat had promised me he would bring me to his house if Kirkuk fell to the Kurdish Peshmerga. The danger of the Kurds taking revenge was real, but not imminent. The imminent danger was what could happen to us during U.S. air raids, and that was what we were thinking about.

The morale of the soldiers was very low. They were the only ones who had to face death, while the officers hid among the reeds on the riverbank at a safe distance from the cannons. They only fired their guns to give orders to attack U.S. planes. During those days, the task of executing soldiers who refrained from attacking the planes was given to the officers and not the firing squad, as they found it was dangerous for them to move between the military positions of our battalion that were under attack.

The soldiers took tranquilizers and painkillers before attacking the planes during air raids. These drugs were the only way they could muster some courage so as to get onto their cannons and fire as if they were having fun. They had hallucinations, and jabbered and laughed. The order to fire was given by the battery unit commander, but the order to end it was out of his control and under the control of the drugged soldiers who, under the influence of the tranquilizers, continued to fire despite orders from Major Yasir to stop. They would only stop when there was no more ammunition, or when the cannon broke down.

Fortunately, they were not aiming at the U.S. planes at all, and were firing at imaginary things they saw in their hallucinations. I feared that they might fire at the neighboring village. After the air raid was over, we had to evacuate the wounded and gather the severed bodies of the soldiers of Republican Guard. The drugged soldiers played and enjoyed themselves by gathering four legs for one dead body, while giving away the body's arms to another corpse. The last thing I wished to happen to me was to be buried by such drug addicts.

Although the U.S. armored vehicles were able to breach through the weak lines of defense around Baghdad several times, I did not expect to hear news of U.S. tanks reaching the city center on Radio Sawa. That day was the end of Saddam Hussein's rule—the ninth of April, 2003. The moment I heard that news I felt a great relief.

It was all over.

There were two possibilities regarding my family. They might have all died under the rubble of our house, especially considering the reports of violent fighting involving tanks in the area where I lived. Or, there might be some of them who had been saved and were free by then, without Saddam Hussein. I was hoping that the fall of Saddam Hussein's statue in al-Firdaus Square would be the end of the nightmare that I had been living for twenty-seven years. Suddenly, I felt at peace.

Fate had finally brought good and bad things to my family, and there was no need to be afraid after that day. I found myself raising my rifle up, pulling the trigger and firing in the air, saluting the city that had fallen. I was happy because of the fall of the dictator, but at the same time I was sad that a foreign army had entered my beloved city.

11

You Are Our Leader, Amer

There was a change in the relationship between the soldiers and their officers. The iron fist of the officers began to lose its grip and the soldiers were no longer wearing their berets or military boots. They did not even care about shaving anymore. Worse, they started to ignore the officers and their orders.

As an example, after the fall of Baghdad we received an order from the battalion to intensify our night watch at the battery unit. That order was useless, as we could seldom find time to sleep since we were constantly moving from one trench to another, and we were tired from carrying munitions and digging holes for shelter. My sleep came to me like seizures, during which I would fall unconscious.

I would fall down out of fatigue and sleep, and sometimes I would not pay any attention to soldiers shouting to me to go to the shelter during bombing raids. They could not force me to run to the shelter; I would react only after the first missile had hit. I remember that one of the officers was standing beside us while we were sleeping in the shelter, and he shouted: "Get up! Go stand guard, the Peshmerga and the Marines are going to take over the battery unit if it's left unguarded."

I said to him, "Sir, the Republican Guards were in Baghdad, and yet the Marines were able to get in. How is it that you want us to protect the battery unit?"

We were not only digging trenches, but had to dig mass graves under the nearby bridge in order to bury our fellow soldiers of the Republican Guard and the infantry who had fallen. We hoped then that these would be temporary graves, and that they would be transferred later on to separate graves where they would be laid to rest with due respect. We could not send their bodies to their families at that time. The reason we chose to bury them under the bridge was because of the spaces on the concrete pillars on which we could write the names of the victims to indicate the presence of a mass grave.

At first, we used to offer the funeral prayers for the fallen soldiers and then bury them. But as the death tolls were rising we were forced to bury them without prayers. We would search their pockets for documents and put them in empty cooking oil containers or glass bottles and attach them to their arms so that they would be distinguishable from the other soldiers in the mass graves.

We also put wood planks from the empty ammunition crates between the corpses in order to separate them. The charred corpses posed a problem, as they were mostly naked and the burnt clothes were stuck to the burnt skin, and the documents were burnt, too. So, we would write on the mass grave that it contained the bodies of such and such soldier, etc., together with three unidentified bodies.

It happened that sometimes we buried a number of victims in a mass grave, and later on foul odors would emanate from somewhere, which after searching we would find was a severed leg or arm or human internal organs. So, as we did not know to whom they belonged, we simply buried them somewhere else.

The digging was an exhausting task, which led us to use the holes that we dug under the bridge for two purposes: sheltering from the bombing and burying the dead after the maneuver was over and we had changed our positions. I remember that once the coalition planes were flying above us, and we had to lie down among the corpses to avoid being hit by shrapnel from the missiles. Sometimes we were so tired that we spent the night in a grave that we had dug for a soldier but could not cover with soil.

The air raids on Kirkuk were ongoing despite the fall of Baghdad. Starting in the early hours of the morning, U.S. planes dumped tons and tons of bombs on the locations of the Fedayeen and the Special Republican Guards forces in Tikrit. Although we had received orders from the battalion, the officers were always giving orders to fire only after the air raid was over in order to avoid being bombed by the U.S. planes, which were raiding the positions of the Republican Guards and the infantry located around us.

Major Yasir did not explicitly talk about that, but it was obvious from his delay firing his gun. I heard the soldiers of the infantry and the Republican Guards swearing at us and cursing us in order to get the soldiers of our battery unit to attack the U.S. planes. Perhaps one of them noticed that our battery unit was hesitating to engage the planes, which led the commander of the battalion to visit us. When he arrived, we heard him say to Major Yasir, "Listen, this is an order, and you have to execute it." And then he went out angrily.

I entered in and asked Major Yasir about what happened. Before I could do so, he said to me, "Amer, tell the soldiers not to move the cannon from its place." Indeed, the soldiers stopped moving the cannon. That was a strange order, because staying in the same location after having attacked the U.S. planes meant suicide. It would be a matter of hours or even less before another air raid that would target our cannons based on satellite images taken previously.

I came to Major Yasir, who was completely confused, and asked him, "Sir, aren't we supposed to leave our location in less than 45 minutes?"

"No, we've received orders to stay here."

"But sir, this means we're going to be targeted by U.S. planes because our location is known."

"I know, but all that matters to the air defense sector now is for us to commit mass suicide in our locations."

"Sir, it's too early to lose hope."

"The air defense sector wants to punish us by making us stay in those locations," he explained, "even though it knows that we're going to be victims of the next raids. One of them has denounced us and the sector is convinced that we are being careless about engaging U.S. planes."

Shortly after, B-52 planes were flying above our cannons. I was extremely afraid, and none of us dared to look at it flying up in the sky. The sight of it was frightening. White smoke began coming out behind the U.S. planes' wings, and then they fired a missile. As it came toward us I felt paralyzed and could not move.

The missile fell into the river. It was clear that that was simply a warning to us to get away from the cannons. So we ran to the riverside, leaving our cannons behind us to be targeted. Minutes later, we saw the heavy cannon which weighed eight tons jumping up in the air and its debris falling onto the positions of the poor soldiers. The planes had completely destroyed our cannon. Major Yasir and I were actually happy with the destruction, as it meant that we would not have to attack U.S. planes anymore.

The U.S. army carried out an airdrop in the Riyadh area, which is an agricultural area to the southeast of our battery unit. They were searching for a pilot whose plane had been shot down above the fields in that area.

I was at the river washing my face when a military vehicle arrived rapidly and stopped. I turned and saw a colonel getting out of the vehicle. I tried to wear my beret so that I could give him the military salute. He did not wait for me and shouted his order at me, "Take your weapon and go to the trenches of the local defense; the Americans have carried out an airdrop operation in the Riyadh area."

He then turned toward some of the families that were living on the riverside and said to me, "Go knock at the doors of these houses and gather the locals."

I carried out what he ordered me to do, and the locals gathered, and the officer addressed them, saying, "The Americans have carried out an airdrop operation in the Riyadh area, and I have been ordered by the First Corps to arm the residents of the area in order to attack the American soldiers."

Then he said to me, "Give the other soldiers this information while I go to the neighboring villages and ask the inhabitants to get ready to fight, and I will provide them with weapons if necessary."

I went to the trenches of the local defense. After the destruction of our cannons we had been assigned the duties of the infantry. We got into the trenches that had been dug previously and which were among the trenches of the local defense. They had been prepared for the soldiers of our battalion should the area be subjected to an airdrop operation. I was afraid of some of the soldiers that were with us: Musa Manahi was one of them, and he was loyal to Saddam Hussein's regime.

I said to him, "Musa, what are we going to do if we are forced to confront U.S. forces? Do we resist and fight, or do we retreat?"

"We will never retreat," said Musa Manahi, and he continued angrily, "I will fight until I die."

"Musa, first of all we are soldiers and we must decide who will be our leader now because there is no officer with us."

Hadi said, "You'll be our leader, Amer!"

"Why me, Hadi? Why don't you be the leader? You're the eldest among us."

"You're a translator and you know the English language perfectly well, and I think that all we need to face the Americans is the English language."

I asked, "Who agrees with this and who disagrees?" They all

agreed. So I said to Musa, "I am asking you once more, if we are faced with the U.S. forces, what will be your response?"

"I'll fight to death."

"Musa, you won't fight. You will already be dead before you pull your trigger."

"Who will kill me, Amer?"

"I will."

Musa was silent. I think that he understood my message. Like most of the victims of the regime, I did not want to resist any force that was trying to get rid of Saddam and his regime, even if it was an occupying force. We did not confront the U.S. forces. They had evacuated their pilot and provided cover for their rescue operation by bombing our positions heavily.

After trying for several days, Major Yasir finally obtained a leave to visit his family in Mosul. He asked me to accompany him to the main road. While on our way, I said to him, "When will you be back, sir?"

"Get back? What are you talking about? I'm not like you, I gave you a chance to escape from this hell when I gave you a leave, and you didn't take it. As for me, I won't let go of it."

We both remained silent until we reached the main road. He bade me farewell saying, "Amer, I hope you'll be saved."

After the fall of Baghdad we were doing almost nothing except going to the shelter during U.S. raids, and burying our dead after they ended. That was why I used to go to warrant officer Abu Hisham's tent. One morning when I went, there were some officers of the infantry with him, talking to him about running away. As soon as they heard the sounds of my footsteps behind the tent, they stopped talking.

I entered without giving the military salute to Abu Hisham. He said to me, "Is this you, Amer? You've frightened us. We thought you were someone else." He then turned to them and said, "Don't worry, he's trustworthy." Then the officers continued with their talks.

They were sitting on the ground wearing civilian clothes, and were thinking about a way to run away. One of them was from Baghdad, and he was deeply worried about the U.S. army's incursion into the city and the Marines patrolling near the Rashad Hospital in the city of al-Thawra. It seemed that his family lived in that area. At that time the soldiers did not have any consideration for military ranks, as if all of them were equal. No one was giving orders, and no one had to execute them. Everybody was only thinking about saving himself.

The soldiers were talking openly about the news of the U.S. forces entering Baghdad and pulling down the statue of Saddam Hussein in Firdaus Square. They were no longer afraid of military intelligence. Although they were shocked by that news, I could understand from their conversations that they were inferring that the opposing sides were on an unequal footing in the war and that the war was worthless.

For example, they were not laying the blame on the Iraqi forces that had been assigned the protection of Baghdad. They were always drawing comparisons between what our units were able to carry out and what we actually wanted to carry out.

In the evening, while the officers were busy trying to find out whether the soldiers were getting ready to flee, and the soldiers were doing the same regarding the officers, we noticed a military vehicle approaching our battery unit. It was a high-ranking officer. He stopped by the side of the river, and asked the soldiers to gather. He then said, "I've come here to bring you good news. Our units will attack Baghdad with chemical weapons, and we will annihilate the U.S. forces there on April 12."

Everyone was shocked by the officer's statement, and I was the most affected by that news. All my family members lived in Baghdad and I feared that they would be victims of that war.

I raised my hand asking for permission to talk and said, "Sir, what about the residents of Baghdad?"

"Don't worry," he assured me before asking, "Is your family there?"

"Yes."

"Don't be afraid. Baghdad has been evacuated completely."

It was probable that the military command would commit such an act, and this could explain the training that we had received from them on using serum against chemical weapons, and the distribution of masks to us before the war. All my worries were for my family. Were they really outside Baghdad, or was the military command lying about this, too?

The overall situation of the army was showing signs of imminent collapse. The coalition forces' incursion into Baghdad meant that everything was over, even though the military leadership in Kirkuk was telling us the contrary. We had to find a solution to our fearful state of anticipation and calmness in Kirkuk.

12

The Escape

Warrant officer Abu Hisham and I tried to find a safe way to escape from Kirkuk. He proposed that we take a military vehicle and go to the city of Dayali, as the checkpoints there seemed easier than the Tikrit checkpoint.

Our plan was to go through the checkpoint several times a day, telling the soldiers there that we were going to the nearby village and were going to return until they recognized us and got used to us.

Our aim was to make the soldiers at the checkpoint believe that we were going to come again. And on the day that the plan was to be executed, we would gather the soldiers of the battery unit onto a vehicle and cover them with camouflage netting and cross the checkpoint, relying on the soldiers' trust in us.

Next morning, Abu Hisham and I, only the two of us, went by the vehicle of the battery unit hoping to cross the checkpoint and return in order to build trust between them and us. Surprisingly, we were not allowed to go through the checkpoint at all, and they ordered us to return back to where we came from.

I woke up at ten o'clock on the morning of April 11. The day before, I had been awake till late in the night and sneaked into the office of the battery unit and took a flashlight, a compass and three guns. I was thinking that we might need them if we had to escape from Kirkuk on foot.

It was a day like any other, or so it seemed. I took the binoculars and began looking in the direction of the checkpoint, which was located to the west of our position on the road linking the cities of Kirkuk and Tikrit. The checkpoint consisted of a building that housed the offices of the Iraqi police and the military police. The strange scene that I saw through the binoculars was surprising; I saw huge numbers of people crossing the checkpoint on their way to Tikrit.

They were moving quickly through the checkpoint without being delayed or searched, contrary to the other days when the soldiers at the checkpoint would take a long time before letting anybody go through. I felt that something out of the ordinary was happening that morning. I woke up the soldiers who were with me and told them we should go to Abu Hisham's location, as it could be that something important had happened.

Abu Hisham's location was three kilometers away from ours, and we set out toward his place. We were surprised to find out that the vehicles of the infantry that had been parked on the road between the checkpoint and our location were not there.

We arrived at Abu Hisham's location; we did not see any officer of the infantry. Lieutenant Qays was not at his location; and we did not see the soldiers of the infantry who used to be at their locations close to ours. Abu Hisham, too, was not to be found at his location. At the time we reached him, he was at the radio set's location.

I asked him, "Abu Hisham, where are the soldiers of the infantry and the officers?"

"Don't ask me, Amer. I've been trying to contact the battalion for half an hour, without any response. They could've been hit by an air strike that destroyed their radio communication location."

Abu Hisham was trying hard to establish contact with the battalion, which had its office twenty kilometers to the north of our locations, in the middle of the city of Kirkuk, whereas our locations were on the southern limits of Kirkuk.

There was another possibility as to why the battalion was not responding to our calls: the advance of the forces of the Marines and the Peshmerga, from the north toward the center of Kirkuk. If they reached far enough, the office of the battalion would be the first of our positions to fall into their hands.

I asked Abu Hisham, "Well, where are the soldiers of the infantry?"

"I heard them moving during the night, and I thought they were changing positions and moving to others in Kirkuk, or that they were moving to Tikrit. I don't really know why they were moving."

The soldiers of the battery unit were like pupils in a school without a teacher. Some were playing football, others were picking fights with others, while a few of them were aware of the magnitude of the danger that we were facing as we were without news about the battalion.

That small group was waiting for me and warrant officer Abu Hisham to give them information about what was happening. At that moment we saw a vehicle approaching us rapidly, and when it came near I noticed that the driver was Major Adnan, the officer in charge of food supplies.

He stopped the vehicle, stepped out and asked for Abu Hisham.

"I'll inform him right now that you're asking for him"

Abu Hisham came, and the officer did not wait to exchange military salutes and said these brief words to him, "Take the soldiers to a safer place." Abu Hisham asked what Major Adnan meant by those words. The major replied with tears in his eyes, "The war is over. Take the soldiers to the other side of the river and make sure you follow the Iraqi military command."

"Sir, with all due respect, I am supposed to take orders regarding military operations from a field commander, and not from you. You are an administrative officer in charge of food supplies."

"What military command do you want to be contacted by regarding the retreat?" replied Major Adnan angrily. "We don't have any military command in the battalion, or the fourth sector of the air defense, or even the whole of Kirkuk."

He paused for a moment, and then said, "We have taken it upon ourselves to give orders to retreat from Kirkuk."

"And who are you, sir?"

"We are a group of low-ranking officers who have taken the responsibility to verbally inform the remaining soldiers in Kirkuk of the retreat, considering that the commanders had fled during the night."

We were stunned by that news, and Abu Hisham asked what had happened to the commander of the battalion.

"He fled last night, and he's the one who sent his personal guards to seize your vehicles in the night."

"I thought there was an order from the command of the artillery brigade to take away the vehicles from the battery units. I could not imagine that the reason was to prepare for the protection of the battalion commander and the high-ranking officers so that they could escape by night."

"This is the reason behind the disappearance of Lieutenant Qays. He informed the battalion commander of your failed attempt to flee by the vehicles last night. That's why the battalion commander decided to take over the vehicles in order that he might escape along with his officers, before you could do that."

It was obvious that the Iraqi army in Kirkuk was going to collapse. All that warrant officer Abu Hisham was concerned about was clearing his responsibility regarding the hundreds of ammunition crates and light weapons such as machine guns and pistols.

He was hoping to get an official document proving that he had submitted the weapons. I think that he did not expect that battle to be the last one; perhaps he thought that it was like what had taken place in the year 1991 when the army collapsed but the Saddam regime remained in place and did not fall.

Major Adnan said to Abu Hisham, "Don't worry about the munitions. Leave them where they are. Just make sure that the soldiers carry their light weapons with them, as they could need them on their way to Baghdad, because all the positions around us are now under the control of either the Marines or the Peshmerga. The Iraqi army has broken down and there's no one there who will ask you about the weapons and the munitions." Then Major Adnan got in his vehicle and took off rapidly toward the city of Tikrit.

On the order of Abu Hisham, the soldiers gathered, and he told them that they had to carry munitions and combat weapons and that they had to form small groups; one group consisting of soldiers living in the city of Mosul, another one consisting of those living in Baghdad or the southern cities.

Abu Hisham stressed the necessity of the soldiers' remaining in groups, as they could come across Iraqi firing squads, the Marines or the Peshmerga on their way, and staying together might give them a better chance of survival.

At that moment I was afraid and anxious about the possibility of being targeted and killed by the Marines from a distance before we could surrender to them as prisoners of war, or that the Peshmerga would carry out revenge attacks against the Iraqi soldiers, or that we would fall into the hands of the Fedayeen, who would force us to fight on the northern borders of Baghdad. It was well-known that whoever was caught by the Fedayeen running away from the battleground in Kirkuk was brought to the northern borders of Baghdad, and was given two choices: either die by summary execution or fight the Americans in Baghdad.

I still had my radio set with me, which was by then my only source of information. While moving from one station to the next in search of news, I heard one of the radio stations saying that the Iraqi army in Kirkuk had collapsed, and the Marines and the forces of the Peshmerga were advancing toward Kirkuk. I did not think about anything except that I was hoping that my mother was not listening to the radio at that time.

The soldiers' reactions to what they heard were mixed and strange. While Sinan was completely shocked, Hadi was aiming his gun at a plastic bottle trying to shoot at it. Hazem the cook was the weirdest of all. We were busy with our weapons and were gathering the munitions, and Hazem was going from one location to another gathering the soldiers' boots and military uniforms, which were distributed to them before the war started. He put the boots and the uniforms in a big sack and carried it on his shoulder even though it was heavy.

He was unlike the soldiers, who were thinking about what could help them survive and was light, so they carried only their weapons with them. Was Hazem thinking that we would join the army again? Or was he thinking about selling the uniforms and the boots he was carrying on his shoulder? Most of the soldiers, whose ages were not above 19, were rejoicing. They thought that they were going to be saved and would get rid of military service. I was thinking that they might not be able to survive and leave the battlefield.

Some soldiers took off in the direction of the northeast toward Mosul, while some of my friends and I took to the southwest toward Baghdad. Although there were reports that Kirkuk had fallen, we still thought until that moment that the Fedayeen and the Ba'athists were at the checkpoints, and that they would execute us should we fall into their hands.

It was an ordinary scene to see a group of Fedayeen tie up Iraqi soldiers and execute them. So we were careful and crawled in the fields of wheat and barley toward the checkpoint. I looked through binoculars to be sure of the precise location where we were moving. I began to get a closer look at the checkpoint, and saw that there were no Ba'athists, military police or Fedayeen there. Indeed, none of them were there; the checkpoint was just an empty building with an Iraqi flag fluttering above

Hundreds of people completely overwhelmed by fear were crossing the checkpoint. The main road was overcrowded with Arabs whom Saddam Hussein had given enticing financial rewards to settle in Kirkuk where the Kurds lived. All of them were fleeing; children, women, men, the elderly, out of fear of the Peshmergas' reprisal. Some were barefoot, others wore bedclothes. There were many stray children crying in the middle of the road.

The main road was not packed with just the Arabs fleeing Kirkuk, but huge numbers of soldiers fleeing Kirkuk, some running and some walking, while the wounded ones were crawling. There were U.S. planes bombing military positions in the distance. The scene was like the Day of Resurrection; language and ordinary words were not being used. People were not talking, they were screaming. I tried to talk to some of them, but in vain. All of them were rushing in one direction: the city of Tikrit.

As soon as my friends and I were sure that the road was safe, we mingled with the fleeing crowds. There were some dead bodies lying on the road, some with traditional Arab clothes on, while others were in military uniforms. I was surprised, when I stood at the corpse of a huge man in his fifties around whom some soldiers had gathered.

"It's General Ihsan Qasem!" I shouted. I stood at his head and really felt avenged by his death, but at the same time I had a feeling of deep sadness. I was told by a soldier that the general had been driving a new model vehicle, and a group of young soldiers who seemed to be his personal guards had forced him out and executed him on the street.

I was riveted to the ground close to the body of General Ihsan Qasem, commander of the security department of the First Corps, when I was suddenly brought back to myself by gunshots. The Peshmerga forces had arrived. It was surprising that they had reached the southern borders of the city of Kirkuk so rapidly. The men of the Peshmerga were firing their truck-mounted machine guns. They were not aiming their guns at us, but were shooting in the air in order to frighten us and make us leave the city.

We were still a group of fifteen fleeing soldiers accompanied by warrant officer Abu Hisham. The strange thing was that Abu Hisham was always trying to walk alone and was keeping himself quite at a distance from us. I think that he was trying to break away from the group so that he might get a better chance of getting a vehicle and leave the city of Kirkuk, because in those circumstances it would have been impossible to find someone who would help fifteen fleeing soldiers.

Even if our group got a vehicle, it would be targeted by the Marines if they were spotted as it would be thought to be a vehicle transporting Iraqi combatants. Abu Hisham hid among trees or mingled with the moving crowds in order to hide his tracks from the younger soldiers and disappear from their sight. The soldiers were running behind him like children trying to catch up with their father.

Despite all of Abu Hisham's attempts, the soldiers knew that he was trying to run away from them, and from his military responsibility of leading them until they reached their cities or villages.

We were at a point on the main road where it branched off into three other roads: The Kirkuk-Tikrit road, a road leading to the villages of Huwayjah, and Riyadh, and a third one which I did not know. It was impossible for us to take the road leading to Tikrit as it was completely under siege and under constant bombing. Also, it was expected to become the scene of wide-scale military operations, being the birthplace of Saddam Hussein and possibly the alternate Iraqi capital after the fall of Baghdad.

As for the road to Huwayja and Riyad, it was under the Marines' control. So, we had no other option than to take the unfamiliar third road. I was not thinking much about that, as my preoccupation was to get out of that region, especially as rumor spread that the Kurdish Peshmerga were approaching. We stopped on the road and, unexpectedly, a small bus stopped. We got in, and the driver drove off rapidly.

"Where can you take us?" I asked.

"I don't know. Any suggestions?"

"Take us to the city of Duz," we suggested, which was one hour away by bus.

"It has been captured by the U.S. army," said the driver.

"Take us to the Daquq area, then."

"It's under the Peshmergas' control," said the driver.

We were afraid to come face to face with the U.S. forces, as they could think that we were going to attack them, and they would target us if we went toward them to surrender ourselves, or we could be attacked by U.S. aircraft. We also feared that if we were captured we could end up like the prisoners of Guantanamo. We could stay for a long time without any trial.

The war on Iraq was, as the U.S. claimed, part of its strategy to fight terrorism, and they could designate the POWs of the Iraqi army as terrorists. The best solution for us was to run away from the U.S. army, as well as from the forces loyal to Saddam Hussein such as the Fedayeen, the Ba'athists or other apparatuses of the state. We were in a confused state because of lack of information, and we did not know which place was safe so that we could go there.

The bus driver shouted at us, "What kind of army are you if you don't know where to retreat?"

The driver then looked at us compassionately and said, "Is it conceivable that the Iraqi army has been defeated to that extent? Is it conceivable that Saddam destroys it like that and runs away and saves his skin, and leaves these young men to be taken as prisoners or killed?"

He was talking to himself with pain, and in a loud voice, and then he said, "We will reach a secure village in ten minutes, and I'll drop you there and I'll leave. Try to sort things out for yourselves in the village."

Indeed we arrived at a secure and peaceful village located near a tributary of the Zab River. We were walking alongside the river, and there were hundreds of Iraqi soldiers walking alongside it too, in the Basateen area. They were walking through the palm trees in order to avoid being spotted by U.S. planes. We joined them, even though we did not know where they were going.

Then we heard sounds of heavy fire, and missiles came flying over us and landed in the crowds of fleeing soldiers, or against trees and exploded. The torn-off bodies of the soldiers were scattered everywhere, and those who were still alive were running in fear. A regiment of the Fedayeen forces was behind us, launching RPG rockets toward the soldiers who were fleeing in order to force them to move forward.

As we arrived at the end of the Basateen area, we saw groups of soldiers running back toward us. They said that the U.S. army was firing on them from the front. The aim of the Fedayeen was to force the soldiers to move forward and fight the Americans. Instead of fighting themselves, they were firing rockets at the fleeing soldiers to make them fight, which resulted in the death of many soldiers from the Fedayeen's rockets.

The Basateen area was ten kilometers long. While one end was under the U.S. army's control, the Fedayeen controlled the other, and they were attacking anyone wearing military uniforms that came toward them. The soldiers' situation was like being "stuck between a pair of pincers," as they say.

There were dead bodies, military uniforms and military boots floating in the river alongside which we were walking. The water had turned red with blood. Insignias of various military ranks were floating on the surface of the water; ranks of captain, general, colonel, lieutenant; all the ranks and uniforms representing the various divisions of the Iraqi army.

The soldiers were throwing their uniforms away so that if the Marines advanced toward them, they could surrender themselves to them as if they were civilians. I saw the soldiers going toward the river and throwing their uniforms in it, and they were wearing civilian clothes under their uniforms, just as I did as a precaution. I was expecting that we would be defeated and that we would need those civilian clothes. I found it was time to get rid of my uniform, so I took it off and threw it in the river.

I found about 175 thousand Iraqi dinars in my pocket, which was the salary of two successive months, and at that time it was worth one hundred U.S. dollars. It was a high salary for a soldier in the Iraqi army at that time, as the military command had distributed generous amounts of money as salaries for the soldiers.

After I had taken the money out of my pocket, I started to throw it in the river, which prompted Sinan to say, "We could need this money; why are you throwing it away?"

"Saddam is everywhere, even as death is approaching me. I see his image in my pocket." I felt agitated by those bank notes bearing the picture of Saddam Hussein.

As we were throwing our clothes in the river, we saw a huge convoy, and one of the military vehicles stopped. It was the convoy of Vice-president Izzat Ibrahim al-Douri, who was responsible for the northern front. He stepped out of the military vehicle and looked at the fleeing soldiers, and then got into the vehicle and drove off in his huge convoy, leaving behind the soldiers who were under his responsibility, and under the responsibility of Saddam Hussein's military command.

13

Homecoming

The fleeing soldiers from Kirkuk were surrounded by U.S. forces and the Fedayeen. We were waiting by the side of a small tributary of the Zab River, hoping that the U.S. forces would be faster to advance toward us. Like the other soldiers, I thought that being taken as a prisoner of war by the U.S. army was better than being arrested and killed by the Fedayeen.

Our wait did not last long, as the Fedayeen started to fire mortar shells toward the area we were in, which resulted in the death of tens of soldiers. We could not move forward as the U.S. forces were targeting everything that moved in their direction. It was a real slaughter. The river was the last resort for escape, and the soldiers began throwing themselves into the water.

The group of soldiers I was with tried to cross the river at a point where the water was not deep. When we reached the other side of the river, we began to run until we arrived at a village whose inhabitants were all Arabs. We asked them to transport us in their vehicles, but they refused to give any help without something in return. That was contrary to our expectation that the Arabs' qualities of extending help and protection to refugees were still prevalent.

We went to the sheikh of the tribe and asked him to help us, and he said, "What will we get in return if we bring you to your destination?" We proposed to give him our salaries, which he refused. He asked for our weapons that we were carrying with us. In fact we agreed that one of the villagers would transport us in exchange for one of the Kalashnikov rifles that we were carrying.

The driver took off with us and drove through an agricultural area, and after some distance he stopped and said, "This is the furthest place I can go." We persuaded him to take us further. Time and again, he stopped and forced us to give him more rifles. Abu Hisham was able to make the driver take us as far away as possible by sometimes giving him a machine gun, sometimes a magazine of ammo. I think Abu Hisham would have given him all the rifles to keep him with us.

I said to Abu Hisham, "I won't give him any other rifle, even if it means we'll have to go on foot."

"What's the use of us keeping the rifles if we're going to die?" replied Abu Hisham.

"We will need them to fight the Fedayeen if they try to kill us."

"Are you crazy to say such a thing? They represent the government."

"What government, Abu Hisham? Everything has fallen apart. And now we have to stay alive even if it means resisting the government."

The driver left us in a plain, where there were a few damaged buildings, an airstrip and huge military vehicles used for transporting troops. There were charred bodies of soldiers inside the vehicles, which were piles of metal debris that had burnt and melted with the soldiers. I also saw two burnt-out helicopters used for airdropping troops. I think these soldiers had been gathered here in preparation for an airdrop somewhere and were bombed by U.S. planes.

They were yet another group of soldiers who had fallen victim to the stupidity of the Iraqi army commanders. It was not a good military tactic to gather the soldiers in that place exposed to the U.S. aviation, especially given that there was no air defense unit that I could see around that airport.

We traversed the airport area on foot and arrived at a small river. We tried to cross it but were surprised to see a man on the other side. We were afraid that he might be a Ba'athist, so we turned back and ran. But the man shouted at the top of his voice, "Don't be afraid, my children. You are safe, don't be afraid. Cross the river and I swear to God that I won't tell anybody that I saw soldiers crossing the river."

We were very afraid of the man informing the Ba'ath party about us, especially since we were going through an area close to the city of Tikrit. The inhabitants there were naturally among those who were most loyal to the regime of Saddam Hussein. That was why we kept away from the residential areas and the inhabitants. But we had to cross the river, as we had no other option.

The man addressed us saying, "Are you soldiers of the First Corps?"
"Yes," replied Abu Hisham.

"I think that Fate has decided that the Iraqi army be defeated every
ten years, and its soldiers return back on foot." The man was referring
to the defeat of the Iraqi army in Kuwait. He added, "What is happening to you now has happened to me before. I returned back from Kuwait
to Baghdad on foot in the year 1991. How long will our army be a play-
thing in the hands of Saddam which he throws into the pits of hellish
and comical wars?"

The man insisted on accompanying and helping us, as he was feeling compassionate toward us. He showed us the right way to go so as
to avoid being caught by Ba'ath party members. He also stressed that
we should take precautions while going through a village on our way,
saying, that there was a powerful and influential Ba'athist organization
in the village.

He then gave us the name of a friend of his, and showed us the
way to his place, saying that the friend would help us. We walked for
about two hours before we arrived at that friend's place. He was an old
man. He welcomed us as guests and offered us food. We were so tired
that we could not eat at all.

We took some food with us, and then the old man took us in his
truck. While he was driving the truck he said to me that he had a son
in the army in the province of Basra who was a lieutenant. He no longer
heard from him and had received no news about him until that moment,
so he was helping the soldiers here in the hope that the God of the Uni-
verse would put someone in the way of his son and help save him.

The man brought us to a place and stopped, and he said, "You can
take this road and it will lead you to a checkpoint at a crossroad which
separates the provinces of Tikrit, Samarra and Kirkuk."

Indeed, we reached the checkpoint located on a roundabout from
which three roads branched off. There were soldiers waiting like us, and
there were about three hundred of them who were all from units based
in Kirkuk. While we were waiting, we were surprised to see several
vehicles, some civilian and others military. There were armed men wearing civilian clothes who came out of those vehicles. They had a Tikriti
accent and were of different ages; some of them were not older than
fourteen years.

There were adolescents who wore military helmets along with traditional robes. Some soldiers began to run away, but there was nowhere
to run as people were coming toward us from every direction. We did

not know where they came from, and we did not notice them coming at all. We did not have time to use our weapons against them, and they started swearing at us. One of the adolescents slapped Hadi on his face and then they took our weapons. They savagely beat the soldiers with the butts of the rifles and machine guns they were carrying.

Abu Hisham and I approached an old man, who seemed to be their leader or the oldest among them, and said to him, "We are not running away from the war, but we've been ordered to retreat by a verbal order from an officer in charge of food supplies."

We were hoping that because of his old age and life experience he would understand our situation, but he replied very nervously and angrily saying, "Do you think Saddam Hussein is over? Was he neglectful toward you? Didn't he provide you with weapons and munitions and vehicles? Do you think that Saddam Hussein has been overthrown? We will dig a hole for you now, and bury all of you in mass graves."

They took Sadeq and Khalid away to a nearby hill. I could hear both of them imploring not to be executed, but to no avail. They tied them up to a power pole and shot them. I stood, frozen, and I knew that they would execute us one by one. At that moment, a small pickup truck came with a machine gun mounted on top of it, which an army officer was controlling. As soon as the group of armed men signaled the vehicle to stop, the officer began to fire at them, which sent all the soldiers running away from the checkpoint. I saw that it was an opportunity for me to save my skin, so I ran with the fleeing soldiers without stopping and we escaped certain death, leaving behind the two corpses of Sadeq and Khalid Hanoon.

We ran continuously until we came to some farms owned by Vice-president Izzat Ibrahim al-Douri. We got into the farm, as we could not walk on the main road, which was strewn with the corpses of soldiers executed by the Fedayeen, who patrolled the main road and executed any soldier who was retreating, even if he was in civilian clothes.

We had no feeling of hunger or thirst, or even sleep. We wanted to save ourselves and to reach somewhere safe far away from the city of Tikrit, and from the men supporting Saddam and his military command.

We reached the farm's end and cut the barbed wires and crossed over to the other side, which was another main road. It was sunset, and the sky was splattered with red and dark clouds, as if they were witnesses to what was happening on earth. I was extremely tired, but there was a force that was driving me to survive. That force was that I should not return back to my mother as a dead body.

We saw a military truck carrying retreating soldiers. We beckoned them to stop and they agreed, and we got in. After that the truck had traveled a short distance, it ran out of fuel. We had to look for a nearby gas station in order to refuel so that we could continue our journey. The only station that was close by was located in the city of Dur, which was the birthplace of Izzat al-Douri, Saddam Hussein's vice-president.

We entered the city of Dur, which was still under the control of the Iraqi army and the Ba'ath party. Out of fear of being spotted by Ba'ath party members we entered the city through minor roads instead of the main road. We sent a soldier in civilian clothes to find out whether the station had fuel, and he returned to tell us there was no fuel there. We took the same minor roads and returned to the main road. It was getting dark and we were shrouded in darkness, as if it wanted to hide us from the eyes of the Fedayeen.

While we were on the main road, two civilian vehicles stopped and men wearing traditional Arab robes came out. They asked us how we were doing, and whether we were in need of help, as they lived in the neighboring farms and could provide us with whatever we needed. The drivers of the military vehicle were inexperienced young men.

They said that they needed food and fuel so that they could continue their journey to Baghdad, and that they were soldiers retreating from military units after the fall of Kirkuk. At that moment, Abu Hisham beckoned me to get off the truck. I understood his sign, and I got off together with Baha, Sinan, Yasin and Hadi, leaving the rest of the group of soldiers in the truck.

The truck disappeared together with the two civilian vehicles. Then Hadi remembered that he had forgotten his personal bag, in which he kept the letters and pictures of his girlfriend, a hairbrush and a flask of perfume he used despite the harsh conditions of the military. Hadi decided to catch up with the truck in order to get his bag back. We told him that he was crazy and that he would be putting his life in danger if he followed them, but he did not listen to us. He stopped a vehicle and went after his memories inside that truck, and probably his death, too.

Abu Hisham asked me to continue our journey, and I replied that I would wait for Hadi and would not leave him alone. He told me that he had probably been killed by then after having been handed over to the Fedayeen or Ba'ath party members and firing squads. I decided to stay and wait for Hadi and the other soldiers. I stayed alone where Abu Hisham, Sinan, Baha and Yasin left me.

I waited a little, and no one came. I decided to go toward them in the hope of finding them. I walked in the direction of the farms for half an hour, and then I heard shots coming from the farms and voices and screams. I knew that the soldiers had been executed, too. I ran back to the main road.

The vehicles of the Fedayeen were roaming along the road. One of the vehicle approached, and I hid myself among the trees and waited. There was a big truck driving on the main road, and it was not the type of vehicle used by the Fedayeen, even though I suspected it might be one of the Ba'athist's vehicles.

Nevertheless, I took the risk and went toward the road trying to stop it. It was very dangerous for me to stay in that area until morning. The vehicle stopped and the driver stepped out. I asked him to help me reach the city of Samarra. He opened the rear door and I saw tens of soldiers sitting there with their heads lowered.

The driver asked me to get in and remain silent, and to lower my head so as not to be seen at the checkpoints. He then covered the box with a tarp. The driver stopped at the limits of the city of Samarra, and we heard him talk loudly. It seemed that he was talking to armed Ba'athists. We had to jump and run away from the truck, otherwise we would have been easy prey for them. The armed men noticed that there were movements at the back of the truck while we were jumping off it and disappearing into the darkness, and the armed men fired randomly at us.

I ran toward the ruins of al-Malwiyyah, climbed up the winding minaret, and stood at the top. I was looking at the tombs of the two Askari Imams buried there. I needed to cry, and I broke into tears, which flowed profusely.

At that time U.S. planes were pounding the city of Tikrit with bombs. The sky above the city was like a huge fireball. I felt quite avenged and I firmly believed that what was happening was an act of revenge against Tikrit and its residents, who had ruled Iraq for thirty years and brought it to such a state.

I could not stay any longer as morning was breaking. I had to leave Samarra as quickly as possible since it was still in the hands of the Ba'athists. I preferred to leave on foot. I climbed down the ancient minaret, walked through ruins dating back to the Abbasid era, and arrived at the marketplace.

I turned to one of the streets in order to avoid walking in the market. I felt some movement behind me. I turned back and saw a number of Fedayeen wandering in the streets of the city.

I ran away and entered into one of the cafés that was still open at that late hour of the night. As I got in, the owner pulled me into the kitchen, opened a big wooden cupboard and asked me to stay silently there until he closed the café. After a while, the man closed the café and knocked at the door of the cupboard, telling me to get out. I got out.

He asked me, "From where did you come?"

I answered, "I've come from Kirkuk, and would like to go to Baghdad."

"Are you crazy enough to enter the café?" he asked, a look of pure astonishment on his face. "Thank your Lord that no one has seen you getting in here, because a group of soldiers took refuge inside the café this afternoon, and Fedayeen forces came and arrested them and executed them in the market in front of the people."

He asked me to sleep and said that the next day he would take me out of the city of Samarra. Indeed, the next morning he took me out of the city and brought me to the Ad Duluiyah area, and then said to me: "Continue walking through these farms until you reach the limits of Baghdad."

Although I was tired I made my way through the farms. The only thing that was pushing me to take each next step was to return back to my mother safe and sound. It would be unfair for that old woman to lose another one of her sons in her last days.

I finally reached the hills of Baghdad and saw hundreds of civilians trying to get back to the city. They were among those who left it before the war for fear of the fighting. There were small buses carrying those returning, and I was able to get a seat on one such bus. All of the passengers were civilians, and they were calling Saddam Hussein names and cursing the Ba'ath party and its members.

I dared not utter those swear words, and instead I turned my face away toward the road, in order to avoid being forced to nod approvingly to them as they cursed Saddam and the Ba'ath party. I could not believe that Saddam was now a thing of the past in the horrible history of Iraq, and that people dared to swear at him in public. Sitting beside me was an old woman and her daughter, who was fully adorned with jewelry.

The old woman came close to me and whispered in my ear, "I have a request for you, and consider me as your mother. I would like you to accompany me until I reach my house, and I would like you to carry the jewelry in your pocket."

"I will stay with you until you reach home safely, mother. But why should I keep your daughter's jewelry with me?"

"There are thieves everywhere and they take away jewelry that women wear," she whispered conspiratorially. "You look like a poor soldier and no one would want to steal from a soldier."

I was shocked by her words. Was it true that stealing was taking place to that extent in the streets and in broad daylight? We arrived at the Jami'a neighborhood where the house of the old woman was, and I felt compelled to get off the bus in order to accompany her to her house as I promised to do.

I reached her house, and gave her daughter's jewelry back to her. She tried to persuade me to accept her invitation for lunch, but I excused myself and thanked her. All I wanted at that moment was to go to my mother.

I walked in the streets of the city, where everything had changed, even the manners of its residents and their humanity. One of the strangest things that I saw was a religious man standing on the pavement calling people to the Friday prayer—and imploring them to stop stealing. And on the other pavement opposing him were people pushing wooden carts loaded with piles of furniture from government offices.

In the middle of the road, there were vehicles of the Marines driving quickly; the Marines were waving their hands at the people and smiling, shouting one word which I think was the first Arabic word they learnt in Baghdad: "Ali Baba."

I quickened my pace towards home. I entered and saw my mother crying as usual. I sat close to her and said: "You wanted me alive, and here I am back and alive, mother."

14

A Door Ajar

So, the war ended with the fall of Saddam Hussein's regime. But I was overwhelmingly shocked by the acts of plundering and looting of the government facilities. I could not imagine how some Iraqis would destroy their country like that. Before the fall of Saddam Hussein's regime I thought that thirty-five years of dictatorship had destroyed the physical infrastructure of Iraq only, but I was surprised to find out that a large section of the Iraqi people had had their manners and principles destroyed.

Contrary to the picture of celebrating freedom in the streets of Baghdad, which I had drawn in my mind, I now saw the picture of my country as facilities and offices were plundered, and smoke billowed above universities and museums, and even hospitals were set on fire after having been looted.

I tried to gauge the Iraqi people's love for their country, and I found out it was fifty-fifty between those who loved and those who hated, in a completely real-life situation among twelve families living in our street. Six of them were involved in acts of looting and plundering, while six other families stayed inside their homes for fear that their houses might be looted after the government facilities.

One of our neighbors, Abu Mahdi, had rented a house to store what he had looted from the nearby Yarmuk Hospital: medical equipment, medicines, medical beds.

Wajeeh and Riyad, two ex-inmates of the Abu Ghraib prison incarcerated on charges of burglary, had become traders in big power generators which they stole from state facilities.

It was common to see Iraqis who had repainted ambulances

120

A local butcher's stall, with fresh wares on full display.

they looted from hospitals and used them for their private transportation.

The U.S. army played the role of spectators as the acts of looting were taking place. The official spokesperson of the coalition forces, General Vincent Brooks publicly announced that the coalition forces did not plan to perform a policing role in Iraq.

I think that the U.S. forces were going against what is stipulated in the Geneva Convention regarding countries under occupation. The Convention states that the occupying forces are responsible for the maintenance of public order, and the protection of civilians and guaranteeing the functioning of civilian administrative offices. Yet, I understand the position of the coalition forces of not intervening to prevent the looting. It could be that they did not want to enter into direct confrontation with the huge numbers of looters. Or it could be that they preferred to go after the remnants of the Ba'athist regime, and the remaining foreign fighters who entered Iraq before the war, and who disappeared from Baghdad after the regime's downfall.

Acts of plundering and looting were not being perpetrated by ordinary Iraqis only, but by some of the more than 100,000 aggravated-crime felons who were released by Saddam Hussein by his pardon in October 2002. Wouldn't it have been worthwhile if the U.S. forces had taken control of Abu Ghraib prison and other prisons and checked their records and arrested the common criminals? The release of those criminals was a deliberate action carried out by Saddam Hussein, so that in case his regime fell, crime and anarchy would spread everywhere, which is what actually happened.

As a result of what happened, I am skeptical about the democracy that the Americans claim they have come to implement in Iraq. I feel that the U.S. could lose the support of the educated people for its project. Every time I argued with one of the thieves about his act, and said that it would be better to safeguard the properties of the state and to think about Iraq's future under democratic rule, he would reply that this is the kind of democracy that he liked.

Drowned in melancholy, I sat in my house with no consolation for what I saw, except my mother, who was extremely happy because I was still alive.

15

Life in the Aftermath: April–May 2003

April 13, 2003

My Friends

I met some of my friends in Baghdad. Despite the sadness that I could see on their faces, they were happy at the fall of Saddam Hussein's regime. They also tried to find suitable ways to inform me of the death of some of our young friends, who were killed in action or in the residential areas targeted by U.S. bombings as there were some air defense units deployed inside those areas. My friends who were still alive thought that I would break down if they would inform me about the death of three of our very close friends. They did not know that, after having been a companion of death for many long months, I would be surprised if any of my loved ones had not been visited by death.

We sat in the café around a table with four chairs, while before the war we would have joined two tables with seven chairs around them. After some introductory conversations I felt bored. They informed me that Athir, Umar and Safa had died. My response was cold, not more than feeling sorry for my dead friends who were not lucky enough to survive.

My friends' pockets are full of dollars and now it is possible for any one of them to buy a whole packet of cigarettes. Previously, they would organize a smoking party for the group with one cigarette passing from one mouth to another.

Interpreters

Perhaps my inner human feelings have been changed by the misfortunes that have afflicted me. As for those friends of mine who are still alive, they are very hopeful that life will be full of opportunities. One of them has reaped the fruits of his hard work while studying at university, and is working as an interpreter with the U.S. forces, and realizes that the years of study were not in vain as he is working within his specialization. Before the fall of Saddam Hussein's regime, his fate would have been to work in a profession that had nothing to do with the field of his studies.

This is Joe, who has changed his name under the influence of his American friends. He gets a free lift in a Humvee vehicle to his workplace, which is a nearby school that the Marines have taken as their base. He is also influential in getting jobs for his friends. Now Joe talks about his desire to own a car, while in the days of Saddam Hussein's regime he dreamed of buying a dictionary to help him with his studies.

A Volunteer Interpreter

Joe started our conversation by proposing that I work as an interpreter with the U.S. forces. I rejected that proposal since I intend to apply for study at the Foreign Service Institute of the Ministry of Foreign Affairs. Nevertheless, I work as a volunteer interpreter between the residents of my neighborhood and the Marines.

A Dream

The search for Saddam Hussein and his aides is still ongoing. It is amazing that Saddam is now on the run when it was my family and I who were being chased after until recently. I do not bother about what happened before the ninth of April. My aim is to enjoy life in a democratic and free Iraq. The destroyed statues of Saddam Hussein on the roads do not bother me. I see them at crossroads in Baghdad while traveling by bus and I do not look at them, as if they were markers for the graves of the soldiers whom we buried in Kirkuk. I try to forget the injustices that I have been subjected to, and to open my eyes to the dream that has come true by means of the spears of a foreign army.

April 20, 2003

Questions

Representatives from Iraqi political parties have agreed today to meet in order to discuss the setting up of an Iraqi civilian authority. I am pleased with the political activism that has started to spread throughout Iraq. For the first time here, various political parties with different ideologies exist, but they all seem to agree upon building a democratic Iraq, far away from the woes and misfortunes brought about by the previous dictatorial governments. I am at the highest level of my optimism despite the fact that I do not know most of these parties. When I hear in the news that these parties represent all Iraqis, I wonder what is the fate of those Iraqis who have lived most of their lifetime in Iraq and have not left it? Are they unqualified for any political participation in the new Iraq? Do those who have lived in exile understand the preoccupations of their people more than those living in the country? Can they understand Iraq's suffering under despotic and unjust rule for thirty-five years? Why is it that the occupying force is turning its back on the personalities at home? The parties that have announced that they will discuss the setting up of an Iraqi civilian authority were not present inside Iraq during Saddam Hussein's rule. This is normal as all those affiliated to these parties would have been executed.

April 21, 2003

The Political Parties Inherit the Ba'ath Party

I wander in Baghdad and think about these parties. They have come into existence as groups of people simply took over Ba'ath party offices, and these offices have overnight changed into offices for the parties. These buildings ought to be under the control of the new Iraqi state, and not any party or political organization. Or, these buildings could serve as educational centers for youth, or public libraries, or new schools in order to ease the overcrowding in schools. Also, how is it that these parties want to fight embezzlement and corruption that were rampant in government institutions during Saddam Hussein's rule, while armed men from these parties have taken control of buildings that belong to the Iraqi people?

Unworthy Traits

I laugh when I see the posters of the parties that are found everywhere in the streets of Baghdad. The names begin with words that indicate whether they are Islamic or secular parties, but all of them end with the word "democratic." There are also posters welcoming the politicians in exile, which are all written in this pattern: "The People of Iraq welcome Mr. — and pledge to him to build a democratic Iraq." None of those names are familiar to me, and I think they are not familiar to Baghdadis either, and the latter did not welcome them, nor did they pledge anything. As a result of the painful experience with Saddam Hussein, these parties have acquired many unworthy traits such as taking away people's freedom and speaking on their behalf.

Slogans

The thing that I dislike most about these parties is their slogans that are found everywhere on the walls of schools, hospitals and other government facilities. This picture reminds me of the slogans of the Ba'ath party. I wish they would rather repair those facilities than deface their walls. Every day, I see a new slogan defacing the walls in my city, and the next morning, members of another party draw a big "X" sign over the slogan of the party competing against it, and write its slogan on it. When I read their slogans on the walls I remember the days when my mother used to listen to radio stations of the Iraqi opposition broadcasting from outside of Iraq. She would make sure the volume of the radio was low for fear that the sound might go beyond the walls of the house. She used to cry and say:

"When will you come and rid us of Saddam?"

"Mom, stop hoping for that to happen. They will forget those who made sacrifices as soon as they are appointed to their posts. Revolution is planned by smart people, executed by the courageous ones and won by the cowards."

"No, my dear. Don't say that. These people have struggled together with your brother and shared his fears along the years. They will come and avenge his death, and will remove the injustices we are suffering and give us our rights."

Extinct Parties

In spite of the short time since these parties came into existence in Baghdad, I am convinced that they are unfit for leading Iraq. Their political programs are no more than resolutions of their founding conferences in exile, which date back to the eighties of the last century. Most of these programs speak about the main objective of bringing down the regime of Saddam Hussein. I am almost certain that these fat and lazy parties have not held a conference for years in order to renew their political programs, or at least, they did not hold a conference before the fall of Saddam and have not discussed the era after the fall of the Ba'athist regime.

May 1, 2003

A Formal Ending

The U.S. president George Bush has formally announced the end of the war. I feel overwhelmed with joy. This means that the rebuilding of Iraq will begin and that I will not hear bombing of planes or gunfire anymore. I will enjoy a life without fear or anxiety. The U.S. army will leave and return back to where it came from, worthy of our thanks. After that we will have our police and army to provide protection and security for our country.

A Salute

The U.S. planes flying above our houses during the day cause great discomfort to my mother. I see her put a scarf on her head in order to cover her hair and rush outside the house every time she hears the sound of helicopters. She stands and salutes the pilots waving her hand at them. Like most Iraqis, she feels obliged to the U.S. army for having rid us of the Ba'athist regime. I laugh and tell her to have pity on her feet, and ask why she should wear a scarf over her head. She says with a tone of conviction:

"My dear, I'm a Muslim woman and it's not permissible for me to show my hair to strangers."

A Recent Picture

The helicopters fly at night too. This disturbs me during my sleep, but it is better than being awakened by members of the police after midnight and thrown in jail. This is a picture that I have in my mind about the recent past from the regime of Saddam Hussein.

Cooperation

I am busy working as a voluntary interpreter between the U.S. forces and the residents of my locality. The people of my locality are very cooperative with the Marines. They inform the Marines of the piles of ammunition left behind by the Iraqi army when they were inside the residential areas. The youths of the neighborhood help carry the ammunition to U.S. military vehicles, which the U.S. soldiers then blow up in an area not far from the neighborhood. They take me with them so that I can act as an interpreter to the inhabitants, telling them not to worry when they hear the explosions of the ammunition.

Food

Expressions of friendship and love are commonly seen between the inhabitants of the locality and the U.S. forces. Not a day goes by without my seeing the young men of the neighborhood bring Iraqi meals and offer them to the U.S. soldiers, expressing their friendly attitude towards those soldiers. We, the youths, help with cleaning up and controlling traffic, hoping that a new Iraqi government will take charge of providing these services.

Arrests

The neighborhood is calm except for a few times during the night when U.S. forces carry out arrests of ex-members of the Fedayeen. The inhabitants cooperate in the arrest of these people, who were really the executioners of the population. As for the Ba'ath party members, they were divided into groups, some of whom have left their homes fearing reprisals while others have changed their outlooks and wear beards and have joined new political parties. Abu Zeena has joined a Shiite Islamic party in spite of the fact that he is a Sabian Mandean.

May 2, 2003

The Office of the Head of Intelligence

I do not know what led me to say yes to my friend Muhammad's proposal to accompany him to the building of the General Intelligence office in al-Harithiyyah. It could be curiosity or wish to take revenge on the horrible memories of that place; not on the persons of the intelligence agents, as they are enjoying their lives in a neighboring country of Iraq to which most of the members of the security apparatuses have fled. During Saddam's rule, that place was one of the strong fortresses of the repressive apparatuses, and which were always connected in my mind to the words "forced disappearance." It was known that whoever entered this building was erased from living memory. Every time I took the bus to go to college in the past, and passed by this building which extends over a long distance in the heart of the city of Baghdad, in the al-Harithiyyah region, I would automatically lower my gaze to the ground out of fear that one of them might see the hate in my eyes.

I entered the building while acts of looting and plundering were still going on inside, not of its furniture, but of its doors and windows, which were being pulled out from the concrete walls. Records were scattered everywhere. I was shocked by the number of intelligence reports that the agents of the secret service inside the residential areas were sending to this security office. I could not prevent myself from entering the office of the head of the Iraqi Intelligence. I went in and sat on the floor instead of the chairs at his desk, as they had both been stolen.

May 3, 2003

A Dream

On a personal level, I have not yet felt a significant change in my life. My hopes do not end at the overthrow of Saddam Hussein's regime, but extend beyond this to living in a real democratic country, where the chaotic situation would end.

A Tombstone for Ahmed's Grave

We held a symbolic funeral for my executed brother Ahmed, and placed a tombstone over his grave, with his name, date of birth and cause of death written on it. It was impossible for us to do that before the fall of Saddam Hussein's regime.

Freedom

For the first time I hear the Call to Prayer aloud from the minaret of a nearby Shiite mosque. The Muezzin mentions the name of "Ali" in the Call to Prayer, who is the first of the twelve Imams whom the Shiite Muslims believe are the rightful successors to the Messenger

Muhammad as leaders of the Muslims. Oh! The Shias have now begun to mention the name of their Imam aloud in their mosques, while sometimes they were even unable to indicate that they were Shias. Also, there are now walking processions to the shrine of Imam Hussein which take place openly, while they were done secretly in the past.

Unacceptable Vengeance

As a Shia Muslim, it hurts me to see the reaction of some of those who are supposedly following the Shiite tradition, and who have forgotten the principle of tolerance and have taken over mosques which were led by their Sunni Muslim brothers. I see this as one of the ways of taking revenge on the regime of Saddam Hussein by targeting the mosques of the Sunnis. I do not approve of these retaliatory acts. I believe that some people have not understood the fact that Saddam Hussein and his regime have never been Sunni Muslims, and that they do not belong to any religion that calls for tolerance and mercy. Although the Shias were those who bore most of the brunt of Saddam Hussein's despotic regime, and the latter tried to appear like a Sunni regime, like any despot, Saddam Hussein relied on dividing people and oppressing a religious group under the guise of protecting another group. He did this in order to remain in power and have the upper hand on everybody, regardless of their religious denominations or creeds.

A Positive Fatwa

Some Shiite clerics tried to put an end to these wrongful acts perpetrated by some Shia extremists by issuing a Fatwa declaring that such acts are unlawful, and by forcing the Shias to return the mosques back to their Sunni brothers. Al-Sayyid al-Sistani was at the forefront of those who demanded that, in his capacity as the senior Shia cleric. His role in toppling Saddam Hussein was as important as that of the U.S. forces. His order to his followers, who are more than several millions in Iraq, not to hinder the advance of the U.S. forces towards Baghdad, played a significant role in making the task of these forces easier.

Al-Sistani and Muqtada Al-Sadr

Al-Sistani is not the only person to have influence over the Shiites in Iraq. There is another power to be reckoned with, in the person of al-Sayyid Muqtada al-Sadr, the son of al-Sayyid Muhammad Muhammad al-Sadr who had been murdered in Baghdad in the year 1999 as a result of his antagonistic positions towards the Ba'athist regime. The followers of al-Sadr the son are influenced by al-Sadr the father, which is why they follow Muqtada, who is not more than thirty years old, and is not known to be a scholar. He does not hold any religious position either. His followers gather around him not because of their belief that he is entitled or qualified to be a leader, but out of admiration for his father. Al-Sadr's followers are concentrated in some Iraqi cities in addition to the city of Saddam, which was known as the city of al-Thawra before Saddam Hussein's rule. It is one of the suburbs of Baghdad. The followers of Muqtada al-Sadr have changed its name to Sadr City.

May 4, 2003

The Loot Markets

Today I went to the market in New Baghdad and al-Bab al-Sharqi. My brothers and I are jobless because of the economic depression these days. People are not buying or manufacturing furniture, which is the business our family is engaged in. These days there are no shops in Baghdad that are open and selling well except those selling stolen objects from the looting and plundering activities.

Saddam's Clothes

Unfortunately, at the loot markets one can see all the things that belonged to the government and to Saddam and his family members under the very eyes and ears of the liberators. In the market of New Baghdad one can see the furniture from the houses of ministers and presidential palaces, as well as the clothes of "Mr. President of the Republic." A man offers people the chance to wear Saddam Hussein's military outfits in exchange for a fee, and people are wearing those outfits and taking souvenir pictures.

Women's Clothing

The strangest thing I saw at the market was a seller who looked like he was very poor standing there shouting:
"Bedclothes! Bedclothes!"

Out of curiosity I approached him and saw a pile of women's underwear which the man was offering to sell at a very high price. I asked one of the people who were curious like me: "Why is this man asking for such a high price for a pile of underwear?" He replied that this was the underwear of Hala, Saddam Hussein's daughter.

I laughed at the extent of hatred and rancor that the Iraqi people harbor for their ex-president. I think that no one would buy these clothes for his wife or lover; it is just for the sake of revenge on the president who is in hiding.

The Iraqi Army's Weapons

Another group of vendors have spread out commodities on the pavement that I thought no one would be interested to buy after the fall of Saddam. They were selling all sorts of weapons, from sporting guns to Kalashnikovs and machine guns, and even hand grenades and RPG rocket-launchers. One of them asked the arms dealer, "Are you seriously selling these weapons which aren't suited for people to use for their personal protection?"

"Yes," said the vendor.

"Do these weapons function properly?"

"Yes, they're functional. If you want to buy a weapon, I can test it for you on one of the damaged government buildings."

Although the weapons are cheap, the Russian sniper rifle "Dragunov" is being sold at a high price because it is in high demand. It is particularly bought by people from al-Ramadi. Most of the weapons belonged to the Iraqi army and were probably sold by the soldiers for a meal or a lift by car during the retreat.

The Horses of Uday Saddam

All the neighborhoods have turned into marketplaces for valuable commodities worth millions of dollars, like the horses of the stable of Uday Saddam Hussein, stolen from his palace in the Jadiriya region in Baghdad. These horses were unlucky to have fallen into the hands of peasants who are ignorant of their real worth. Some of them used the horses to pull carts and transport harvested crops, which caused many of them to die, especially when their diet was a few vegetables while previously they had been fed with fodder imported from international farms.

May 5, 2003

Paul Bremer

I find it strange that a person whose expertise is terrorism has been appointed as the civil administrator of Iraq. We do not need experts on terrorism. Never was Iraq a breeding-ground for extremist Takfiri (excommunicator) ideologies. Soon the Americans will realize that Iraqis are peaceful and that they have nothing to do with terrorism. However, it is comforting that Paul Bremer's task will be to help Iraqis set up a democratic government, so that the U.S. forces would be able to evacuate Iraq and leave it for its good people to do the reconstruction according to the way they find suitable. We have enough experts in politics, economics and science, which make us competent to take charge of this.

May 15, 2003

The Hawasims (the Conclusive Battles)

Our bad neighbor decided to move to another house today, in the Zayuna neighborhood where only wealthy people live. It seems that our modest neighborhood is no longer suitable for a millionaire like him, who made his living from stealing cooking gas containers all his life.

The unexpected wealth of our neighbor did not affect him alone, but his mother and his wife too. The wife threw all the old furniture of the house away, and she has begun to behave as if she were born to a wealthy family and pretends to forget that she used to wear shabby clothes and mended sandals. Our bad neighbor's mother behaves haughtily towards the women in the neighborhood and no longer greets my mother.

This neighbor of ours was among those who took part in the stealing and looting of the government-owned al-Rashid bank. He was like most of the gang members whom Saddam Hussein released by his pardon prior to the war. Those people have become the richest people in Iraq after having stolen millions of dollars from the looted banks. The Iraqis have given those thieves a name, which is al-Hawasim. This term, which means "the Conclusive Battles," was used by Saddam Hussein to designate his last war against the United States. After the war ended, Saddam disappeared and thieves were found everywhere, and it was common for someone who owned a luxurious car and did not drive it well to be called "Hawasim," meaning that he had recently become rich from his robberies.

16

The Struggle for a New Iraq: May 2003–February 2005

May 22, 2003

The End of the Sanctions

The United Nations issued a resolution today lifting the economic sanctions imposed on Iraq, and gave its support to the civilian administration of Iraq under the leadership of the U.S. I am optimistic about the first part of the resolution but am not pleased with the second part. Although the decision to overthrow Saddam Hussein was basically a U.S. initiative, I wish that countries would set aside their political differences, and that the international community as a whole would work together to find a solution to the Iraqi problem and help us rebuild our country, after the fruitless wars of Saddam Hussein's regime that have destroyed Iraq, and the economic sanctions which have crippled it and turned it into one of the poorest countries in the world, and the most backward country in terms of its economy and services. In addition to that, there were more than one million Iraqi children who died, and whom Saddam and his regime kept in morgue refrigerators at the hospitals instead of handing them over to their families. They would then carry out mass funerals for children in Baghdad from time to time, as a propaganda campaign in the struggle between Saddam and the U.S., while the Iraqis were the only ones to pay the price for that.

May 23, 2003

Army, Media, Ba'ath Party ... and Questions

Today, the civilian administrator Paul Bremer has dissolved the ministries of defense and information, and dismantled the Ba'ath party. That decision has had an immediate and significant impact on us, and Iraqis are asking many questions such as these:

- If we don't have an Iraqi army to protect the borders against intrusions, which army will we seek help from?
- What will be the fate of thousands of those who belong to that army?
- Doesn't Mr. Bremer have fears that the already high levels of unemployment among the Iraqi youths will get even worse?
- Many of those aged between 20 and 35 have become jobless. Doesn't Mr. Bremer fear that these young men could drift towards crime and deviance?
- Disbanding the army and building a new one will take a long time. This means that the U.S. forces will remained in Iraq for a longer period than is necessary. So, when will these forces leave?
- Iraq's borders are long and it is located alongside a group of countries none of which, I believe, support the setting up of a democratic system in Iraq. Also, they certainly do not approve of any U.S. accomplishments in Iraq. Should the U.S. project be successful, these countries are afraid that Iraq could become a model for democratic countries, and that their own people would demand some of the rights enjoyed by the Iraqi citizen. That is why they could interfere in Iraq one way or another. What will we do about this danger?

I was surprised by the decision of the American official to disband the Iraqi army and dissolve the ministry of defense, although I agree with him on dismantling the Ba'ath party and the ministry of information. To me, it was a dream to have freedom of the press without being under restrictions from a ministry. I am also optimistic about the number of newspapers that exist and the diverse opinions that they voice, unlike the situation during Saddam Hussein's era. The press is a real safeguard in order to correct and criticize government's actions in case it does make a mistake. The dismantling of the Ba'ath party was one my greatest wishes. Also, I wonder why no international condemnation

has been issued against the genocidal acts perpetrated by the Arab
Socialist Ba'ath Party against the citizens of Iraq.

July 1, 2003

Democracy at Home

I have discussions with my brothers and my mother in the living
room, and we talk in the light of an oil lamp hoping that the power
will be back and that we will not suffer power cuts, permanent or temporary. The U.S. is a country which is very advanced technologically,
and it can restore electric power in the few coming days, including
power to the crippled Iraqi homes. Such are our conversations and
hopes. We also talk about who we think is appropriate to govern Iraq
now. My choice is Dr. Iyad Allawi, who is a medical doctor and is able
to heal Iraq's wounds. My brothers choose other political leaders. Irrespective of the political or religious affiliations of these leaders, what
we hope for is an impartial government, far away from reprehensible
sectarianism.

July 6, 2003

Language and Clashes

I am looking for a job as an interpreter with civilian authorities. I
do not want to work as an interpreter with the U.S. forces, especially
after the clashes between the residents of our neighborhood and the U.S.
forces. Some boys of the neighborhood threw stones at the U.S. forces'
base. The U.S. soldiers do not understand why the residents of the
neighborhood have turned against them and begun to hate them when
they were very amiable towards them before. I know the reason behind
those clashes, which is that U.S. soldiers inadvertently used improper
words with the residents of the neighborhood. The soldiers had learned
those improper words from some youths of the neighborhood. The fact
that the U.S. soldiers do not know the Arabic language has led to
increasing hatred towards them. There is another reason for the increasing hatred, which is the traffic accidents involving U.S. tanks bumping
into civilian vehicles transporting families. There have also been inci-
dents where U.S. troops would kill people when the tanks came under
fire from unidentified shooters.

Islamists and Communists

I went to Palestine Meridien Hotel in the morning, as it is the place where the international and Arabic media are based. Perhaps one of the media crews would be in need of an interpreter to help them communicate with the Iraqis for their news coverage. The hotel was surrounded by a kind of barbed wire that I am not used to seeing; U.S. barbed wire is different from Russian barbed wire, which has for a long time surrounded everything in Iraq, even our hearts. I was disturbed by the sight of the barbed wire, which I hoped never to see again after the fall of Saddam. Wires are wires, whether they are neat U.S. barbed wires or Russian barbed wires. These wires were between U.S. Abrams tanks on one side, and Iraqi demonstrators on the other side, who were gathered in groups. Some were asking for the protection of the environment, others were asking for the protection of women. The strangest thing was that there were two groups of demonstrators, one of them representing an Islamic party, and they were shouting: "Yes, yes to Islam, No, No to Unbelief, No, No to Atheism."

The Islamic group was shouting its slogan at another group, which responded with another slogan: "A free homeland, and a happy nation."

The people in the group shouting "a free homeland and a happy nation" had tied pieces of red cloth around their arms; they are from the Iraqi Communist Party. I laughed at both of them. They were still obsessed about competing against each other, which they used to do during the times of the cold war.

I think that this demonstration is a show of force meant to convince the U.S. forces that it is this group or that one which has the last word in the public arena in Iraq, and that it is the one which is fit for governing Iraq. The ways in which these parties behave are not simply based on whims, but they have undoubtedly noticed that the U.S. is ignorant of the facts in Iraq and the silent political forces that exist there. I have realized that the U.S. is in need of an Iraqi partner in the project for a new Iraq, in order to clear their image of an authoritarian occupier, and to prove their good intentions about handing over power to Iraqis. However, I do not understand why the U.S. is only interested in the leaders of parties that came back from exile and ignores the local political figures.

July 13, 2003

The Governing Council

I woke up early. I do not want to miss any one of new Iraq's mornings and was enjoying the breeze and the sound of white peaceful doves cooing. I was standing at the door when our neighbor Abu Ala passed by and said, "Enjoy it, Shiites of Iraq! The Americans have offered you 13 seats in the council."

I did not stay awake last night and I missed the news bulletin. What government did the Americans give us, and what seats is Abu Ala talking about? Supposedly, Iraq should have only one seat for the president and another one for the prime minister; as for the rest of the seats, they should be for the ministers. I was angry since Iraq was never America's property to offer to whoever it wanted. I interpreted Abu Ala's words as if he was talking about ministries and allocation of portfolios. I asked him jokingly:

"What seats do you mean, Abu Ala? Has a new government been elected during the night?"

He replied with a tone of anger and dissatisfaction:

"It seems that you haven't listened to the news yesterday. A Governing Council has been formed and the Shias have got 13 seats, although they do not represent the majority of Iraq."

I remained silent and did not reply to our Sunni Iraqi neighbor.

Allocation of Seats

I entered the house and talked with my brothers about what I heard, and I found that they knew what happened last night. Strangely, they were not convinced that the Shias' share was not more than 13 seats, as they wanted more. I asked my elder sister:

"Didn't you choose Adnan al-Baja Jee, who is a Sunni, a few days ago when we were talking about who we wished to govern Iraq? What made you change your mind so that you want more seats for the Shias? Will the Sunni or the Shia be successful in rebuilding Iraq just because he is a Sunni or Shia, even though he is not fit to lead Iraq? Do you prefer that a Shia becomes our leader although he is a dictator?"

"Well, if the situation turns out to be about allocating seats during the night between Shias, Sunnis and Kurds without focusing on competence, I am for the idea of Shias getting a maximum number of seats, even though they are unfit for governing the country."

I understood from my sister's answer that despite the fact that sectarianism is present, Paul Bremer made it apparent for people to see, and made it the policy of the new Iraq. I said that it was a summer cloud that would move on and the sectarian polarization detrimental to Iraq would not continue like that.

July 20, 2003

The Parties' Shops

Some of my friends decided to go to the offices of the political parties which are found everywhere in our region, like vegetable shops. They were hoping to get membership forms for one of the parties, not because they believed in the principles of these parties or in their political programs, but because these parties were announcing that they would provide jobs to whoever is affiliated with them, when they come to power in Iraq. Also, after having obtained their seats on the Governing Council, they began to give the impression to the Iraqis of the various religious denominations and groups that they were the protectors of the rights of this group or that one, and that they were trying to come to power not because their leaders wanted to hold ministerial posts, but because they had pledged themselves to stop the injustices and persecution committed against the followers of the denominations they pretend to represent.

July 20, 2003

They Humiliate Us

I was standing in a long queue which extended from the Adnan Khair Allah club to the gate of al-Muthanna airport, which the U.S. forces had taken as their base. I was there to collect 40 dollars, like the rest of those waiting in the queue, as a compensation for the salary that we used to get in the Iraqi army before the war ended.

Although this amount of money, after being converted into the Iraqi currency, will not buy a pair of trousers and a shirt, it nevertheless helps to solve some financial problems for the thousands of ex-conscripts in the Iraqi army, which has been disbanded by the coalition forces, and whose ex-members are unemployed.

Since morning I had been waiting in the line with others like me under the scorching heat of the sun. I had every hope that my turn would arrive at midday. Like other people, I was vexed by the behavior of some U.S. soldiers who were carrying sticks in order to maintain order in the queue.

I was asking myself, "Why do these soldiers treat us with such contempt, and why do they shout at us and threaten to beat us with those sticks? What would be their feeling should they be in that line and soldiers of a foreign army were treating them in the same way they are treating us?"

Arabs and Iraqis

The attitude of the interpreters working at the Muthanna airport was worse. These interpreters held Egyptian, Lebanese and other Arab nationalities, and their deliberate provocation of the Iraqi soldiers was worse than the provocation caused by the U.S. soldiers out of ignorance.

The Americans have no knowledge of the culture of the Iraqi people, and these two come from cultures which are different from each other to a great extent, whereas the Arab interpreters share practically the same culture with the Iraqis, and in spite of this they intentionally provoke the Iraqis. The Arab interpreters say things of their own accord without limiting themselves to translating what the U.S. soldiers say.

I know this because I am a translator myself and I know what an honest translation means. The Arab interpreters turn to the Iraqi soldiers and swear at them for the most trivial reasons, and threaten them with sticks, too. I felt humiliated by the way the Arab interpreters behaved and the silence of the U.S. soldiers about their reprehensible acts.

I approached a U.S. female officer and said to her: "Be careful of this interpreter, he's not translating what you're saying honestly, and instead he's humiliating us on purpose without you knowing about it." The female officer just advised the interpreter. She probably did not believe what I said to her, because she did not know what her interpreter was saying to us in Arabic.

Ba'athists

There were many Iraqi warrant officers in the line, and they were inciting the soldiers in an indirect way not to obey the orders of the U.S. soldiers. Most of these warrant officers were formerly members of the military office of the Ba'ath party. They were instigating the Iraqi soldiers, saying to them, "It's a shame that you accept being humiliated by the occupier. Look how they're trying to humiliate you."

These words found an echo in the hearts of some soldiers, especially those that were inexperienced and reckless and aged not more than 19 years. And what helped the warrant officers to incite the soldiers was the link between the repressive methods which were widely used to maintain order in the queues at the recruiting camps and the sticks of the U.S. army. There is a strange similarity between the attitude of the U.S. army and the regime of Saddam Hussein, and that was what incited the Iraqi soldiers, as their dream was that their dignity would be preserved after the arrival of the Americans. But as it appears to them now, the situation is no less humiliating than it was during Saddam Hussein's rule.

A Clash of Cultures

I lived one of the worst days of my life. I could not believe that the image of the friendly U.S. soldier would, in the eyes of the Iraqis, turn into the image of an occupation soldier who mistreats elderly Iraqis and humiliates them. But this is what happened today, and it is difficult to understand that change without knowing the preceding conditions and causes that led to it.

An old man came from the end of the line to the head, trying to avoid waiting in this long queue. The young soldiers waiting in the line did not show any objection, as it is known in Iraqi customs and traditions that we let elderly people go ahead of others without asking for permission whenever they want and in any queue whatsoever.

Of course, the U.S. soldiers do not understand this, and one of them approached the old man and tried to return him back to the end. The old man moved nervously and reproached the U.S. soldier for treating him the way he was treating the young Iraqi soldiers. The U.S. soldier pushed the old man and threw him on the ground, and his headband fell on the ground too. The Iraqi soldiers were full of fiery anger.

What the U.S. soldiers do not know is that the headband falling off an Arab's head in Iraq means the loss of his dignity. The Ba'athists waiting among the soldiers in the line exploited that scene to incite the soldiers, who began to pelt the Americans with stones. I realized that the situation would explode, and got out of the line and returned back home before becoming another victim of a clash between cultures.

On TV, I saw the news about the clashes between the U.S. soldiers and the Iraqi ex-soldiers in front of the gate of al-Muthanna airport. One dead and many injured among the Iraqis, and injuries among the Americans. The news report said that the Iraqi soldiers were angry over non-payment of their salaries. This is totally contrary to the facts. The fact is that the Americans do not understand the culture of the Iraqi people. That incident changed the image of the U.S. soldiers in the eyes of the Iraqi youths.

August 21, 2003

Demonstration

Today, we took part in a peaceful demonstration protesting the U.S. forces' appointment of people in our neighborhood, who were corrupt officials in the municipality of Baghdad, as counselors in the new municipal council. We did not expect the U.S. officer to talk to us in order to know what our demands were.

The demonstration was a real experience of expressing our wishes in a democratic way. At first, we were afraid of the reaction of the U.S. forces to the demonstration. The image of the previous Iraqi army and its reaction to demonstrators was still in our minds. We feared that the U.S. forces would fire at the demonstration, which I called for together with some of my friends. I was impressed by the scenes of demonstrations which I saw in American films, and I wished that one day I would take part in a demonstration.

August 23, 2003

The Quest for a Party

I became convinced that it would only be possible for me to render services to my country through collective action, which would work toward realizing shared goals. There was not a more effective way to achieve this other than by joining a party whose members all agree on a particular set of objectives that the party will move towards realizing.

I paid a visit to one of the parties known for its participation in conferences that the opposition held outside Iraq during the days of Saddam Hussein's rule. The person responsible for the cadre of students and youths referred to me as "the cadre leader of the party" in the first meeting that I was present at, even though I had not yet joined the party.

I was asking myself what kind of party was that one which called me cadre leader the first time that I took part in its meetings. I discovered the fragility of that party, which comprised a few dozen members, most of whom belonged to a single family in Baghdad. The fragile make-up of this party was not different from most of the parties in Iraq, both liberal and religious ones. They are "family business" parties.

Family Business Parties

I was sitting with some young men who were enthusiastic about engaging in political activities. We were in a hall which still had Ba'athist slogans on its walls, as the building was previously a Ba'ath Party office. We were having a conversation about political activism and the need to attract the youths to the "principles of the party." I stopped at the expression "principles of the party," which the person in charge said quite shyly.

I said to him, "Sir, there are well-known Islamic parties out there whose ideologies are equally well-known, and such is the case with liberal parties too. So, what are the principles that your party is based on so that I might get to know them first, and afterwards it would be possible for me to reject them or embrace them and explain them to those youths whom I think are suitable to join the party?"

He replied, "Yes, you asked me about the objectives of the party ... errrr." Then the person in charge kept silent for a while. I was convinced then that his party was nothing but a family investment company under the guise of a party, and which would collect membership fees from its members, and try to gain the sympathy of the American civilian administrator in the hope of securing a ministerial post through which the family party could loot public funds.

So, I decided to look for another party.

August 25, 2003

The Universal Declaration of Human Rights

My friends and I try to live out some of our ambitions as youths who are deeply fond of culture and the arts. A group of young men and I agreed to set up a non-governmental organization for the arts and literature and promoting human rights and democracy. The first thing we did was to print the Universal Declaration of Human Rights at our own expense and distribute copies of it in the streets of Baghdad.

We were hoping to participate as youths in spreading ideas about democracy and human rights among the Iraqis, and help our people firstly to know their rights, and secondly to protect them from being afflicted with another dictator who would turn their dream into a horrible nightmare, and who would be difficult to get rid of except by foreign forces. I worked on a voluntary basis and did not intend to work for material gains. My dream was to build my country first.

French Reservations

We tried to organize an arts festival to enable young people to express themselves. We could not find a suitable hall for that festival except the French Cultural Centre hall in Baghdad. After trying for quite some time I was able to meet the French cultural attaché. The man was affable, but he was talking to me with reservation. I told him about our need for the hall of the French Cultural Centre for theatrical and artistic performances. I was surprised by his reply, as he said, "I can't help you. Your country is on the brink of civil war and I can't risk opening the halls of the Centre for you. The security situation is precarious after the assassination of Sergio De Mello."

Let's Depend on Ourselves

The French cultural attaché's words about a civil war among Iraqis were a kind of non-sense. I took his words to mean that he did not want to admit that the U.S. occupation of Iraq has been successful in liberating the will of a number of young people who are now trying to express themselves. The U.S. occupation of Iraq was, in the view of the French government, a unilateral action by the U.S.

I think that France would not welcome any action that would make a project for democracy in Iraq led by the U.S. successful. I did not bother about what the French cultural attaché told me. Our ambitions as young people are too strong for the opposing interests of countries to stifle them. We tried to find a suitable place to carry out our performances using our modest resources only.

White and orange taxis crowd the front of a Baghdad restaurant.

August 29, 2003

A Dreadful Assassination

The Iraqis are holding their breath, fearing that an ethnic conflict might explode after the dreadful assassination of Sayyid Muhammad Baqir al-Hakim. His murder was not just the assassination of a well-known religious figure, but a sacrilege committed against the shrine of Imam Ali Ibn Abi Talib, the paternal cousin of the Prophet Muhammad (Peace be upon Him). This shrine is sacred to all Muslims, and the assassination is a desecration of the Friday prayer which is one of the sacred acts of worship for the Muslims, because it happened during that prayer.

Umm Khalid, who is our neighbor and my mother's best friend, was the one who brought that news to us. We were surprised, and I was more surprised by my mother's response towards the neighbor. She was not loving toward her Sunni Iraqi friend. My mother jumped to her feet, saying, "Hakim did not die. And even if he did die, there's someone to take revenge on his murderers."

My mother was talking in an angry voice to her best friend, as if she was implicitly accusing all Sunnis for being behind the terrorist operation which Sayyid Muhammad Baqir al-Hakim was a victim of. Or as if she was accusing her friend of rejoicing at the murder of this Shiite icon. I hope that the Shias do not harbor the same feeling that my mother has.

I fear that retaliatory attacks against the Sunnis could break out, or that they could be blamed for that criminal act which has afflicted all Iraqis. I have hope in al-Sayyid al-Sistani, being the most authoritative Shia cleric, and hope that the Shias will abide by his fatwa, which calls for restraint and for not resorting to acts of vengeance. There was a rumor spreading among the people saying that al-Sayyid Muhammad Baqir al-Hakim did not die in that incident, and the proof according to what people were saying was that his body was not found there.

October 5, 2003

The University Theatre

We went to the university and met one of the professors. He showed great enthusiasm and really helped us to get permission from the dean of the university in order to organize theatrical and poetry performances in the theatre of the university. The theatre was damaged due to acts of looting and plundering. The thieves had stolen the chairs, the lamps and even the curtains, and despite all this we gave our performances.

An Invitation

Our relationship with the university professor grew stronger and he invited us to attend a weekly meeting that he holds with a group of professors from the Mustansiriya University, and who were then contemplating the setting up of a human rights organization in Iraq.

October 7, 2003

The Foundation of the Human Rights Organization:

Today we held a meeting in order to lay the foundations of an organization for educating people on matters of democracy and human rights. We agreed to rent an office on a commercial street which overlooks the university. Most of the members fall into two age groups, which are the youths, and the older people who are university professors.

I found it difficult to understand the university professors, as most of them were narcissistic and excessively arrogant and were keen on holding positions. They did not believe that there are young people who can take charge of carrying out human rights activities. Besides, they were extremely against the idea of getting funds from sources other than members.

American organizations had offered us financial support, which the university professors refused under the pretext that they fear that those giving their support might influence the types of activities. I disagreed with them completely, because no one in these organizations had given us preliminary preconditions. Instead, they agreed with us that it was necessary that the human rights NGOs should carry out their activities freely.

The Pre-eminent Value

I disagreed with one of the university professors on many of his secular ideas, but I do agree with him on one principle, which is that human rights should be the pre-eminent value that the new Iraq upholds. Among these rights is the right of the people to directly elect their government, and the abolition of the sectarian quota system which was implemented in the setting up of the Governing Council, and which Paul Bremer was probably forced to resort to.

I think that the U.S. was greatly in need of an Iraqi body to which it could hand over power. But I wonder whether the U.S. would give power to someone even though he was not suited for it or had no legitimacy originating from the ballot boxes.

October 10, 2003

Embezzlement Activities

The U.S. forces started their reconstruction activities in the neighborhood, such as the restoration of schools and clinics. It was announced that the municipal council appointed by the U.S. forces was undertaking these projects in our neighborhood. I worked on one of those projects of reconstruction, which was not more than painting the school buildings and the clinics. Those supervising me at work did not know that I knew the English language well, and that enabled me to discover what was happening in the shadows.

For example, I heard a conversation between a U.S. officer and an Iraqi contractor from the municipal council of our neighborhood. The contractor was talking about the cost of repairing the school, saying that it was fifty thousand dollars. The U.S. officer did not object as he was completely ignorant of the prices of raw materials and labor costs in the Iraqi market. The contractor did not do anything except paint the walls of the school, which probably did not cost more than two thousand dollars. The name of the municipal council has become connected with stealing, and its members, appointed by the U.S. forces, have turned into a bunch of wealthy thieves.

Do the American taxpayers know where their money goes?

October 21, 2003

The Assassination of Dr. Zaki

In the morning, I was surprised by my friend Muhammad knocking violently at the door. I opened the door and saw him crying. He told me, "Change your clothes quickly, we have to pay the last honors to the doctor today."

I asked Muhammad, "Has Zaki died?"

"The doctor was assassinated, after having given his opinion about the future of Iraq, and criticizing the new Iraqi politicians on one of the Arabic satellite channels."

Bullets and Coffins

The professor was a victim of his belief in the right of the people to criticize the politicians and to voice their opinion freely. It seems that fear will not leave us alone even after the fall of Saddam Hussein's statue in the Firdaus Square. The problem is that the one who assassinated Dr. Zaki is unknown. Is it conceivable that nothing has changed in Iraq?

The coffins are the same, and the bullets are the same, but those who shot them are unknown. This is contrary to what it was like before since we knew that the previous regime was the only one which bathed in the blood of the Iraqis. But today, the door is open for all kinds of speculations.

October 23, 2003

Rumors and Wealth

I feel hopeful again. After a meeting held by eighty donor countries, they said that they will help Iraq rise from its economic stagnation. There was a rumor saying that Iraq would become another Hong Kong, and that the oil revenues will be distributed among the Iraqi people. If this happens, we will become a rich nation because of the rise of oil prices in the world market.

I think that oil-producing countries are behind the destabilization in Iraq and are targeting Iraqi oil pipelines, in order to get Iraq out of the oil market so that it will not compete against them and become the second ranking country in the world in oil production.

October 27, 2003

The Terrorists Target the Red Crescent

I was shocked by what happened today. The terrorists have targeted the office of the Iraqi Red Crescent. What is the advantage to them in carrying out such a cowardly act? The Red Crescent is an institution which helps the Iraqi hospitals by providing them with medicines and medical equipment.

The lack of medical equipment is a consequence of the looting and plundering activities which the hospitals suffered after the fall of Saddam Hussein's regime. I lost one of my dearest friends in one such terrorist act. He was Nawwar and he graduated from the translation department of the faculty of arts, like me. He could not find a job in his specialization, so he worked as a security guard at the office of the Iraqi Red Crescent.

November 6, 2003

Keys

I have been trying to contact the members of the human rights organization for many days, in order to prepare for another meeting and to resume our activities. I paid a visit to one of the university professors at his office. I found him confused and afraid. He did not agree to attend the meeting, fearing that he might be killed, as the previous president of the organization was killed.

He reached for his pockets and threw a bunch of keys at me, saying, "These are the keys of the organization's office. Go there and remove the signboard from the front of the office. We have to reduce the activities of the organization these days."

The Heirs of Saddam

I was shocked by the university professor's cowardly and defeatist attitude. We were not engaged in any activity that was in opposition to anything. It was just a peaceful activity aimed at spreading the principles of human rights which the politicians brag about and which they consider to be among the most important things that their parties uphold. What is there to be afraid of?

Although I knew that those Iraqi politicians were lying, the picture was clear to me since the beginning. The Iraqi politicians, including those who opposed Saddam Hussein for thirty years, make use of the same tactics that Saddam used. They suffer from the complex of megalomania and rejection of differing views, and they attempt to suppress them, if not stifle them by using force. I could not find any excuse for someone who would try to spread the principles of human rights secretly and covertly. The first right we have to claim back is our right to freedom of expressing ourselves publicly.

November 21, 2003

The Professors Did Not Come

Even though many of the professors agreed to attend the meeting at the office of the organization today, most of them did not come. My friends and I held the meeting. There were just five young members present. We agreed to hold the foundational conference of the organization in the beginning of the next month, so that members from outside of Iraq would be able to attend it.

December 13, 2003

The Capture of Saddam Hussein

We were stunned while watching the TV in the living room. Is this really Saddam Hussein? Is it true that he has finally been captured? Is this man with a thick beard and a dirty outlook the one who was the cause of our misery and fear, and the destruction of our country for thirty-five years? Though some in our family were speculating and having doubts about what they were seeing on the TV screen, my mother said, "This is him, I swear to God! I can never make a mistake about identifying him. It's him, with all his moves and facial traits."

It was indeed Saddam Hussein with all his moves and looks. He seemed broken while the American doctor was examining his teeth and hair. To us, Saddam was after all just one picture which fell off the list of fifty-five names of people holding positions of power in Saddam Hussein's regime, and whom the Americans want to bring to justice. There were heavy gunshots in celebration of Saddam's arrest. I do not expect terrorism to end in Iraq with his arrest. Anyway, the day Saddam was captured was not an ordinary one.

December 20, 2003

Disappointment

The foundational conference was held today in the conference room of the union of engineers in Baghdad. The attendance level was high, which was unexpected especially after the assassination of Dr. Zaki, and since most of the professors had been afraid to attend the preparatory meetings. The foundational conference was nothing but disappointing.

It focused on criticizing the U.S. forces instead of focusing on building a new Iraq. They surely have the right to criticize whoever they want, which is what happens in all the countries that care for human rights. But wouldn't it have been better to focus on the necessity of holding elections in order to elect a government to which the U.S. will hand over power, instead of just focusing on criticizing the U.S. forces? Had we had an elected government ready to take over the reins of power, we would not have needed a foreign army in our country.

Another Disappointment

The academics living outside of Iraq for a quarter of a century have nominated one of the professors as the president of the human rights organization, without presenting his name along with others' names to the members for them to elect the president in a democratic environment. What happened was a true representation of the absence of democracy within an organization promoting democracy.

No sooner was the professor's name mentioned than the rest of the professors agreed to that, without paying attention to our objection to the nomination of the president of the organization in such a shameful way and without any election. Dictatorship is not ingrained in the political parties only, but has also pervaded the NGOs which are working to spread democratic values

An Attempt

We, the youths, decided to retain our membership in the organization and attempt to correct the shortcomings by promoting democratic practices from within.

March 2, 2004

A Call for Help

Ambulances and police vehicles are driving around in the streets of the neighborhood where I live. They are calling everyone who can go to the al-Kazimiya hospital to go there and donate blood. The hospital is overcrowded with injured persons, and blood donors help meet the shortage of blood.

Carnage on a Sacred Day

I have just returned back from al-Kazimiya hospital. I came back feeling tired after having donated blood for the victims of the bombing which took place this morning in al-Kazimiya. There was a similar bombing in Karbala. Today is the Day of Ashura, which Muslims of all sects celebrate, and they fast on that day as a way to get closer to Allah. It is also the day when Imam Hussein was martyred in Karbala in Iraq.

What happened today in al-Kazimiya and Karbala was unexpected; suicide bombers blew up themselves and their explosives-packed vehicles in the middle of crowds of Shia Muslims who were commemorating the martyrdom of Hussein. More than 180 Iraqis have lost their lives and there were hundreds of others who were injured. Although I knew that there are extremist Salafis who consider us, Shias, as unbelievers, I could not imagine that their level of extremism would lead them to kill. I could not imagine that a Muslim, whatever his sect, would find a religious excuse to kill innocent people on a sacred day like this one.

Abu Mus'ab al-Zarqawi

The U.S. military command in Iraq held the group of Abu Mus'ab al-Zarqawi, who is a Jordanian, responsible for both the massacres in al-Kazimiya and Karbala. Sectarian tensions have started to emerge in Baghdad and among its inhabitants. I notice this mostly in the evening while traveling by bus and listening to people talking. The politicians are exploiting the situation to campaign for their ideas and their parties, most of which are based on sectarian principles. That was not surprising as these parties lack popular support and I think that they have started to sow the seeds of sectarianism.

March 31, 2004

American Contractors

Four American contractors have been killed in the city of Fallujah. Their bodies were dragged in the streets of the city and they were mutilated. Under the corpse of one of those who were killed they found a paper which read: "Falluja is a graveyard for the Americans."

Falluja is located in the region known as the Sunni triangle, where Saddam Hussein enjoyed a strong support. The sight of the mutilated bodies of the four American contractors is reprehensible. I cannot find an explanation for the barbaric treatment that these corpses were subjected to, and those who murdered these contractors and mutilated their bodies are crueler than starving beasts.

A Statement That Was Not Issued

Today I tried to issue a statement on behalf of the human rights organization which I am a founding member of, but to no avail. My friends in the organization feared for their own safety in case the organization were to issue such a statement. My response to my colleagues' attitude was clear. There was no need to be afraid of issuing a statement condemning that barbaric act which took place in Falluja. Defending human rights demands courage and self-confidence. But in spite of this, the statement was not issued.

April 4, 2004

Clashes and Victims

More than forty Iraqis have died as a result of the clashes between the supporters of al-Sayyid Muqtada al-Sadr and the U.S. forces in Baghdad, Basra and Najaf today. I did not expect that any Shiite group would enter into confrontation with the U.S. forces, because the Shiites are the first ones to benefit from the presence of these forces. Without them the regime of Saddam Hussein would not have collapsed, and his nightmarish rule over not just the Shiites, but also the rest of the Iraqis, would not have ended.

What happened today was not unexpected. Afterwards the coalition forces issued a ruling to shut down the al-Hawza newspaper, which belongs to the supporters of Muqtada al-Sadr. They also arrested Moayyid al-Khazraji, one of the most prominent supporters of al-Sadr the son; he was also one of the supporters of al-Sayyid Muhammad

A typically crowded Baghdad market.

Sadiq al-Sadr the father. Al-Khazraji is also one of those who fell victim to Saddam Hussein's oppression.

The Americans Did Not Understand

I wish the Americans understood the nature of al-Sadr's supporters, and the successful and effective ways to hold them back. Most of the youths are aged between 16 and 30 years, and they come from poor and densely populated areas which lack basic amenities like drinking water and sewage disposal. Most of them did not complete their primary education. This is what differentiates them from the supporters of al-Sayyid al-Sistani, who are educated adults. The U.S. forces would have been able to hold the supporters of Muqtada al-Sadr back had they promptly provided the amenities and jobs.

April 29, 2004

The Fear of Foreign Fighters

I returned back home feeling tired. I was at the refugee camps in the Jami'a neighborhood in Baghdad during most of the day. The camps were set up to accommodate the displaced persons from the city of Fallujah who have left their city because of the battles taking place between the U.S. forces and the foreign fighters for the last month.

Though the inhabitants were denying the existence of these fighters in their city, I confirmed that they were there while talking to some child refugees who came with their families to Baghdad. I asked a little girl whose name is Hiba whether she saw foreign fighters in the city of Fallujah and she affirmed that she saw them, but her father quickly grabbed her away to the camp. Afterwards, I heard her crying. Maybe she was beaten by her father. The inhabitants of Falluja avoid talking about the existence of foreign fighters in their cities out of fear of those fighters.

Separation

The situation in the camps is desperate. No aid is reaching the refugees except aid from the Red Crescent and the food and the blankets that some Iraqis are giving out. Most of the families are scattered. We go from tent to tent and take the names of these families and search for their lost relatives by distributing their names to the nearby schools in Baghdad. During the past days we were able to reach some of the missing children, who were in the custody of Iraqi foster families, and we returned them back to their families. I wonder, how long fear will be the most prominent attribute in our children.

Abu Ghraib Scandal

U.S. soldiers scaring naked Iraqi inmates in Abu Ghraib prison with dogs and forcing them to mimic sexual acts. Human rights violations in Abu Ghraib prison which have been exposed by the pictures of the Iraqi inmates have greatly tarnished the image of the U.S. soldier in Iraq. These pictures that we have seen today have changed the image from that of a liberating soldier to an occupying soldier who humiliates Iraqis.

It has also badly affected the concept of democracy, which the U.S. claimed it has come to bring to Iraq. The U.S. soldier is no longer viewed as a defender of freedom and human rights now that these pictures have been seen, and the concept of democracy which the U.S. forces have brought to Iraq is now called into question.

May 11, 2004

The Fear of Terrorism

As usual, I was the first to arrive at our organization's office. We were supposed to meet in order to talk about issuing a statement which we have hesitated to issue for a long time denouncing the human rights violations which took place in Abu Ghraib prison. We ought to be defenders of human rights and the first ones to stop the violation of these rights, irrespective of whoever is behind these violations. But I found out that the university professors wanted our organization to defend human rights with the least effort possible and in ways that will keep it away from terrorism, which we know is the *real* violator of human rights. The organization limits itself to criticizing the U.S. forces' violations of human rights inside Iraqi prisons because they know that the U.S. forces would not confront an organization in the field of human rights.

A Hesitating Statement

I strongly supported issuing a statement that would condemn the human rights violations in Abu Ghraib prison and would include a clause condemning the beheading of the American hostage Nicholas

Berg. One of the professors preferred that we not criticize his murder in order to avoid any response from the terrorists and what they could do to the organization and its members. Although I insisted on criticizing the reprehensible killing, the statement made only a hesitating reference to Nicholas Berg's execution.

May 28, 2004

Iyad Allawi

The Governing Council has appointed Dr. Iyad Allawi as the prime minister of the interim government which will take over power from the American civilian administrator Paul Bremer on the thirtieth of June. The roles of the American civilian administration and the Governing Council will come to an end.

June 2, 2004

Tourist Professors

One German organization offered us an opportunity to participate in a training workshop on human rights and election monitoring. We found that it was a good opportunity, especially given that elections are going to be held soon in our country, and we are very much in need of trained persons to monitor the ballot boxes. I was surprised when the university professors of our organization presented names of persons who had joined the organization just today.

They are all relatives or acquaintances of the professors. I think that the professors have accepted their membership in order to legitimize their participation in the training workshop to be held outside Iraq. I said to one of the professors, "Those persons whom you intend to bring with us in the training workshop are all your friends or relatives, and they've only joined the organization today."

The professor replied, "These persons teach at the university and they hold high degrees." In fact, I could not see any relationship between their being academics and the fact of being involved in human rights activities. It is known that human rights are not tied to a particular academic position or a specific social group.

I wondered, "Is this a human rights organization or a travel and tours company?"

I left the office and returned back home while they were busy preparing for their recreational journey.

June 5, 2004

Youths and Academics

The young members of the human rights organization have agreed that we will participate in the training workshop, and that we will later set up our own human rights organization that will not include the academics. Its objective will be to train people who truly believe in the principles of human rights so that they may take part in monitoring the elections in Iraq. We have also arranged with an American organization to finance a project which our newly-founded organization has come forth with, which is to train 480 persons to monitor the elections.

It would be impossible for us to make such an arrangement if we remain members of the present organization, especially because the academics refuse any financial support from American organizations. They say they are afraid that the financiers might control their activities. But the fact is that they are simply people who have a phobia about everything that is American, especially given that most of them used to be members of the dismantled Ba'ath party.

Several times I had discussions with those obstinate people about cooperating with American organizations, but to no avail. I could not find one single reason for their hatred of everything which is American other than their previous political affiliations. They hate those who have stripped them of the privileges which they used to enjoy during the previous regime's rule.

June 17, 2004

Jordanians

We were invited to the Jordanian capital, Amman, two days ago by a Jordanian organization working to promote human rights in collaboration with the German organization which is funding the training workshop. The aim of the lectures was supposedly to train us on how to promote human rights and monitor elections.

In fact, the workshop was nothing but discussions about Iraq and the illegitimacy of the U.S. military intervention which overthrew Saddam Hussein's regime. Once again, there was antagonism towards the U.S. Also, Saddam Hussein and his regime are glorified in Amman. This is the opinion held by the Jordanians whom I met in Amman.

I said to them, "My dear friends, we are here today in order to receive training in election monitoring, and not to praise Saddam or to criticize America. Saddam is a dictator and I am thankful to the U.S. forces because they have rid the Iraqi people of him."

No sooner had I said these words than hell was unleashed upon me. The Jordanians disapproved of my stance. Even though Jordan looks, to the outsider, like a country which enjoys an acceptable standard of democracy in a region ruled by cruel dictatorships and repressive police states, an inside observer will see a country ruled by secret police. I have noticed the presence of members of the Jordanian secret police at the training workshop, and I found their presence at a workshop on human rights strange.

June 28, 2004

The Interim Government

I am happy at the Americans' handing over power to an Iraqi interim government, but I am not at ease with the method used by the U.S. authorities to appoint Dr. Allawi. The right to choose the prime minister and the government should belong to the Iraqi people and should be exercised by means of free elections. It seems that this is not possible now. There must be an elected parliament which would enact laws on the electoral process.

July 1, 2004

Saddam Hussein Appears Before the Judge

I am very happy today. Saddam Hussein was shown on TV sitting in front of a judge in his first appearance in court in order to hear the charges of genocide and war crimes against him. Saddam Hussein did not recognize the legitimacy of the court and accused President George Bush of being the real criminal.

I am amazed by how things have developed over time. Before, Saddam was a tyrannical ruler who condemned hundreds of thousands of people to death and millions to perpetual torture. Now, he is in front of a judge who is representing all his Iraqi victims.

A Prediction

I remember a song by the singer Fu'ad Salim who has migrated abroad, in which he says:

I swear by you, Ghaida
That we shall take back our due rights
And we shall try him in the desert.

When I heard that on the opposition radio station, I thought that it was some kind of wishful dream that would never come true. Today, I think of it as a prediction which has come true. Indeed, I am thankful to the U.S. army.

July 20, 2004

At the Gate

I woke up early today in the hope that I would be among the first persons to submit their applications at the Foreign Service Institute of the Ministry of Foreign Affairs. This institute trains the diplomatic personnel to work at the Iraqi embassies abroad. During the rule of Saddam Hussein I used to dream of studying at this institute. At that time it was just a dream and nothing more because of the regime's stance towards my family.

Today, the situation is different. The Ba'athist regime in Iraq has been overthrown, and the new government is determined to treat everyone equally and give the sons of Iraq the opportunity to build their country far from any considerations based on sectarian or political affiliations. I arrived at the building of the Ministry of Foreign Affairs, which housed the office where applications for joining the Institute are submitted. I stood in a long line in the sun which melted my brain but not my hope of reaching the gate of the ministry.

While I was standing there waiting for my turn to arrive, I saw new luxurious cars stopping near the gate. Young men of my age stepped out of them, carrying the same forms used for applying at the Institute, but they did not wait in the line like us and instead went straight towards the gate, talked to the guards and entered in. They appeared to be the sons of the new politicians. Their fathers want them to inherit their political positions in Iraq after these politicians who came from outside of Iraq retire.

Who Is Your Father?

Finally, I reached the gate, and they allowed me in for an interview with one of the professors of the institute. The interview consisted of a number of questions on politics. I answered them all and did not make any mistakes. I lived in a house where the only thing that we talked about was politics and politicians. It seems that the professor was kind to me and wanted to spare me from facing the harshness of reality.

He asked me, "Is your father an exile politician?"

"No, sir," I replied. "My father was a peasant and he never left Iraq."

"Are you a Kurd?" asked the professor.

"No, I'm an Arab," I answered truthfully.

"So," he responded, closing my file, "don't waste your energy. The seats of the institute are reserved for Kurds only, and those who have high-level connections."

Job Quotas

I went to the office of one of the political parties which I thought was impartial and had a patriotic program not based on dividing the Iraqis according to their ethnicity, or sect, or who your father is.

I entered the party's office and said angrily to one of the officials, "Have we paid for our freedom with nights spent in gloomy prisons while those coming from abroad enjoy the fruits of our efforts?"

"Calm down," he said. "What has happened?"

"They do not want to accept me at the Foreign Service Institute just because I am not a Kurd and my father is not a politician who came from abroad," I explained.

"Don't be angry," he told me. "If you are dreaming of getting a job, take this application form for a job in the Ministry of Health. This Ministry is under the control of our party, and you will be able to start working there as of tomorrow morning."

I was shocked by what this politician was saying. It seems that his mind sees no difference between someone who is looking for a job and someone who *wants* a job, which he thinks is most suited to his abilities and qualifications in order to serve his country.

An Oath

I left him and got out, and swore that I would never work in a Ministry where all the employees are from a particular political party.

August 27, 2004

A Crisis in Najaf

For three weeks supporters of Muqtada al-Sadr have been fighting. They have taken the shrine of Imam Ali in Najaf as their stronghold. They are trying to cause embarrassment to those Shiites who do not support this reckless youth in his hazardous attempts to drag them into a confrontation with the U.S. forces.

There are fears that the shrine might be damaged as a result of the skirmishes between Muqtada from the Mahdi Army, and the U.S. forces. Then the Shiite genie might pop out of the bottle and Iraq could turn into a fierce battleground between the U.S. forces and a new player who has remained silent and supportive of the political process in Iraq. He represents the overwhelming majority of Shias who are supporters of al-Sayyid al-Sistani in Iraq. Even worse, two hundred million Shias around the world might revolt, and these people are also supporters of al-Sayyid al-Sistani, and they are found in countries from Afghanistan, Pakistan, India, and Iran to Lebanon and Iraq.

A Red Line

Al-Sayyid al-Sistani has declared that the city of Najaf is a red line that all those involved in the conflict should not cross. Thanks to God, the situation did not explode and was kept under control by al-Sistani's wisdom once again. His mediation was very helpful in preserving the dignity of both sides.

The supporters of Muqtada al-Sadr were under siege inside the shrine of Imam Ali, and they were surely going to be defeated, and it would have been embarrassing to them to surrender themselves up. As for the U.S. forces, they would have been able to win this battle militarily, but the cost of this victory would have been very high as they would have lost the support of the Shias, especially if they fought the supporters of al-Sadr inside the shrine of Imam Ali. Al-Sayyid al-Sistani's mediation was a fair solution. The supporters of al-Sadr have surrendered their weapons and have been spared from legal action being taken against them.

September 1, 2004

An Iraqi James Bond

Being a human rights activist brings a lot of trouble to me, especially when the people in my city discover my efforts. They think any person who is working in this field is a traitor trying to apply a Western agenda through human rights principles. In the past two weeks I have felt insecure in my city, and my house is not a safe place for me to live in any longer so I contacted my friend Sinan, who works in a training camp for the Iraqi Special Forces. He agreed to take me with him for an interview for a job as an interpreter in a U.S. camp where the Iraqi Special Forces undergo training.

We had to take different taxis to reach the camp. We took a taxi from one place to another in order to avoid being tracked by someone, because Sinan had disclosed that he works at a U.S. camp and had received threats telling him to quit the job or else he would be butchered. Sinan's moves clearly showed his anxiety, and his behavior was similar to characters in American adventure/detective movies. We were like individuals who were on a secret mission, like James Bond's missions.

The Fear of Being Denounced

We arrived at the camp and the guards at the gate searched us thoroughly. They were Filipino guards who were guarding the camp where a U.S. company training the Iraqi Special Forces is based. We reached the waiting area where Sinan kept trying to sit behind the parked vehicles as if he were hiding himself from some people. I asked him why he was doing that.

He explained, "Many of those who work in this camp are Iraqis, and I fear that one of them might come from the neighborhood where I live. He could recognize me and talk about me in the neighborhood."

I thought his fears were understandable. In fact, the unexpected did happen. After waiting for an hour, the security company in charge of providing security and protection at the camp changed shift, and among the guards was Thamir, a resident of my neighborhood. I know him as a good person but I feared that he might see me and tell his mother about what he saw. She is known to be the most gossipy lady of the neighborhood.

The Prayer of Fear

I prayed silently not to have to wait for long there. Sinan called an American woman on his cell phone and informed her that we had arrived. She assured him that one of the American training officers was on his way to bring us inside.

A few minutes later, a car stopped near us and I saw an American training officer in civilian clothing, wearing a helmet and a bullet-proof vest, and carrying an M-60 rifle and a pistol. It was the first time that I rode in a vehicle with an armed American. The training officer was dealing with me in a cheerful and kind manner, and he tried to calm my fears about the interview by cracking jokes.

An Agreement

An American woman in her mid-forties carried out the interview with me. She spoke Arabic very fluently. While talking to Sinan, I came to know that she was the one who had spoken to him on the phone. We agreed that I would start my job on September 14, that is, after two weeks. I would work as an interpreter between the U.S. training officers and the Iraqi Special Forces who were undergoing training.

September 4, 2004

Translators Chased by Terror

After much thought, I informed my family that I have decided to leave Iraq on September 14. This was, of course, to keep my work as a translator with the Americans secret as I would be absent from home for months. I had an agreement that I would stay in the camp and not leave. My family would not have agreed for me to work with the Americans, not because they are against working with them, but out of fear that the terrorists might discover that I work with the Americans and kill me.

Expectations that this might happen were high, especially knowing that every morning one can find a dead translator who used to work with the Americans in the streets of Baghdad. And usually the body was beheaded with both hands tied behind the back. I have gone through the dreadful experience of losing many of my friends who graduated with me from the translation department of the faculty of humanities. Despite my mother's sadness at my departure, she felt a little relieved, because she thought that I was going to travel far away from Baghdad, the city of death.

September 1, 2004

My Dear

I woke up in the morning and took my bag, ready to leave. I did not know how long I would be away from home, because after all that has happened in Iraq, one can no longer plan anything further in time than the step one is going to take in the next second. I bid my family farewell.

They were sure that I was going to leave Iraq, and it never came to their minds that I would be just a few kilometers away in the camp close to our neighborhood. The funny thing was that I forgot to act as I should, as my mother came running after me in the street, her eyes filled with tears, and shouting, "My dear, you've forgotten your passport."

I kissed her and said to her, "I was overwhelmed with sadness, which made me forget my passport."

A Compassionate Look

I went to the main road, and as Sinan used to do, I took several taxis which drove me through all the neighborhoods of Baghdad before reaching the U.S. camp. I did not do that only to get out of sight of anyone trying to track me. Traveling through the neighborhoods of Baghdad was a chance for me to have probably a last look at the city where I was born and where I wish to die.

The Translators' Tent

I arrived at the camp. The woman who was my immediate superior gave me a bed in the translators' tent. She relieved me of any work for that day.

The Greatest Translator

I was sitting in the tent thinking that I was not going to work today as my supervisor told me, when the Man of the Fog (that was a nickname of one of the translators in the camp) came to me and asked me to accompany him to the educational halls where trainers lecture.

When we reached there, he asked me to wait outside the hall. I hadn't started my work yet in the camp by that time as a translator. I hadn't waited long before an American trainer advanced towards me and started talking in a Texas dialect.

He was muscular and tall. To be more accurate, he was too much like stars of action movies produced in Hollywood. After introducing himself, he asked me to be his interpreter for his lecture that day. I became confused, because I wasn't ready to start work that day. When I confessed my fears, he said, "If you're not ready, why are you here in this place?" I didn't find a way out but accepted so as not to lose my work.

I came into the class where there were 24 students; all of them were glaring at me. The lecture was about security measures in the shooting range. The trainer was speaking fast with long sentences of which I could hardly make out anything. Irrespective of all this, I tried to go on with my translation. Confusion was clear on the faces of the students while listening to me translating interrupted, meaningless sentences. It was clear that military terminology used in the shooting range is the same found in dictionaries, but the controversial point is that the idiomatic meaning of the words couldn't be translated but by a specialized translator who is familiar with these terms. I was only specialized in human rights translation.

I went on with my translation. When my confusion went from bad worse, I started to translate the questions of the trainer as separated phrases only. The trainer waited for responses to his questions in vain. The students didn't understand my translation. Anyway, I started to answer the questions in different ways than that of the trainees. While they preferred silence, I kept telling the trainer to shed more light on certain points. I kept doing that till a complete hour had passed. In the break, I went to the students and told them that it was my first day and that I hoped they would not report my translation mistakes. I asked them to say "Yes" each time the trainer asked them if the point was clear. They did what I wanted. Every time the trainer asked them if the point was clear, the students said, "Yes."

This encouraged the trainer to finish his lesson. I was relieved. He then told me that he wanted to speak to the students to build friendly relationships with them. He started actually to speak to them. He told them jokes that I understood, but I wasn't able to convey their content that was full of American cultural names such as the fast food restaurants and words with double meanings.

In that way, students were not able to understand the translation and so it was not funny for them. This situation left the trainer showing signs of reluctance on his face because of my poor translation. To find a way out, I was obliged to ask the students to break into laughter as soon as the trainer had finished telling his joke. At the beginning, they were producing affected laughters, but later they were taken by something like a laughter attack because of this situation. After he finished, he looked at me and said, "You're the greatest translator I have ever seen in my life!"

First Night

My first night was very quiet in the first hours when I was stretching on my bed, enjoying moments of relaxation after a day that was full of translation mistakes. While I was lying on the bed with headphones in my ear, listening to the band Queen and my favorite song "Another One Bites the Dust," trying to escape with my soul outside the camp walls, I was surprised to see translators rushing out of the tent.

I preferred not to follow them or ask them about the reason for their running because I didn't want to mix with translators at the beginning. I was afraid that my acquaintance and friendship with them would lead to conversations from which they could know my true identity and my residence. While the sound of the Queen drummer was going on, I saw a group of trainers running in front of the tent with their helmets and armor on. I said to myself, "It must be something dangerous." As soon as I had taken the headphones off my ears, I heard the sound of other drums that I will never forget in my lifetime. It was the sound of mortar missiles!

I ran out of the tent quickly, following the running trainers until we reached a cement building, and entered it after them. The cement refuge was overcrowded by translators, trainers, and different workers in the camp. I couldn't help laughing when I saw one of the translators trying to cover his body, which was covered only by soap bubbles in some parts. It seemed that the poor guy had been taking his shower and had not been able to put on his clothes when the sound of the missiles burst into the bathroom. This situation recalled to my mind the flashbacks of the war that I lived, and raised a question inside myself: "Why should you keep running among the blasts that shake your skull?"

A few minutes later, I heard the sound of choppers hovering in the air. One of translators said, "Everything is over. The Apache helicopters will scan the surrounding area." Although translators and workers started to move out of the refuge, I preferred to stay for a while after seeing the remaining trainers inside the refuge. However, I was obliged to go when the senior trainer asked me to accompany him to the trainees' rooms to assure himself about them.

When we advanced towards the trainees' rooms, the smell of smoke coming out of mortar missiles filled the air. One of the trainees wondered whether I had been afraid or not. I said, "I'm afraid as a man, but I'm used to such situations and even worse." It was totally different being bombed by B-52s and by normal mortar missiles that may hit or miss their targets.

When we reached the rooms of the soldiers, they were waiting outside, but I didn't know why. The trainer asked them, "Do you feel down after the mortar missiles?"

They answered, "No."

They even pretended to have absolute courage by standing outside the concrete building, not paying attention to the missiles and the fragments. Their way of talking to the trainer was too far from the truth. They told the trainer something and told me the contrary. When I asked them about what happened during the bombing, they spoke about acrobatics and circus moves they did when the missiles started to pour into the camp.

The camp corporal had stuck himself in the AC opening when he heard the impact of the first missile. Now he experienced contusions not from the effect of missile splinters, but from the effect of the fear that penetrated his heart because the sound of the missile after he stuffed himself in the ventilation opening.

November 10, 2004

Translator 83

He was in the prime of his youth with a thin and tall figure and wore vitreous eyeglasses. He used to spend his days working, and his nights playing video games. After escaping an unfruitful attempt to bomb his house by armed guerrillas in Baghdad, he adopted the American camps as a new house. "Translator 83" was a model for an entire generation of youth that had carried their life burdens since early age. He worked to support his mother and 10-year-old sister after his father fled the house one day, leaving his poor son to settle the debts of the fleeing father.

"Eighty-three" seems now as if he is a big child to the extent that anybody sharing his tent is forced to play the role of the father in everything, especially hygiene. His smell is unbearable, especially because he used not to shower unless he was forced or was threatened with being deprived of sleeping in the tent for one night. Each time he finishes his shower, his fellow translators make a dancing party for him.

"Eighty-three" was born in 1983 and that's why we used to call him "83." Speaking to him one time about life and its burdens, I was surprised by his strange experience in life despite his young age. He worked one day in Abu Ghraib prison, wearing a mask to hide his identity while working as an interpreter for American investigators who were questioning robbery suspects. Ironically enough, his own father was among those suspects who were accused of the stealing and spoliation crimes that overwhelmed Iraq after April 9. "Eighty-three" was obliged to change his voice pitch and dialect to imitate an Egyptian man so that his father couldn't identify him. "Eighty-three" broke into laughter after he had finished talking about that day. The smile on his face showed a feeling of rejoicing over his father's misfortune.

Sushi and the Man of the Fog

Translator Sushi looks in his late thirties; he is married and has children. He is among those translators who spend their weekend with their families while they spend the other days of the week either working or drinking heavily with the other translator called Man of the Fog. However, Sushi is the kind of man who makes you think he is a straight Muslim who adheres to Islamic law, which prohibits wine. You can tell that from his persistence in prayers. I asked him more than one time about this behavioral paradox between his adherence to Islamic religion and drinking wine.

His unchanged answer was, "Allah will punish me for drinking wine and I will ask Allah to forgive me so my sins and good deeds will be equaled and then I'll enter paradise." The truth that he wanted to say, but he didn't, is that his drinking wine was an escape from his reality while his prayer represents his fear of death. Every time Sushi leaves the camp to visit his family, he wears old stained clothes to convince the dwellers of his suburb that he works just as a construction worker.

Sushi is a name selected by his trainers though he has never tasted real sushi in his life. Trainers used to call the translators funny names, perhaps because they wanted to add a sense of humor to their hazardous work in Iraq. As for the translators, they didn't object to that because they have long looked for false names to hide their true identities and they may have wanted to share their trainer's sense of humor, too.

The Man of the Fog was named after London, the City of Fog, which he has never been to, but he convinced his family before working in the camp that he was going to travel to London to work there. He lied to them to hide the nature of his work. Because his family believed that he was in London, his fellow translators called him the Man of the Fog.

When the Man of the Fog was going to visit his family, he left the camp in the company of the trainers to go the PX to buy gifts for his family so that they would completely believe the story of his traveling to London. What is funny in this story is that is family used to meet him with shouting, clapping, dancing and singing to express their delight and pride in their son coming from the City of Fog.

December 17, 2004

I Don't Trust My Fellow Citizens!

The senior trainer asked me to meet him in front of the trainers' rooms. I had already met him with my helmet and full armor on. On seeing me he stared at my face, went into the tent and came back with a mask. He ordered me to wear it so that no one could identify me! We got into the trainer's car, which was followed by a group of other armed trainers, rushing on the road. It seemed as if they were going to join severe fighting.

To break my astonishment, the trainer told me that we were going to receive a new wave of soldiers that we were required to train in our camp. Instead of going to the waiting area, he turned to the outer gate leading to outside the airport. It is a place where the bullets of terrorist snipers and RBG missiles can reach easily. Recognizing his wrong path, the trainer turned his steering wheel quickly to avoid advancing farther into the targeted road. He then reached the entrance gate. Once I recognized the situation, I felt real fear. The gate is subject to strict inspection done by Iraqi workers who are supervised by a Western security company.

I was scared that they might ask me to take off my mask. I

expressed my fears to the trainer. He reassured me. He asked me to remain as calm as possible and not to utter a word. Actually, I had nothing to do but to follow the orders of the trainer. Reaching the gate, the Iraqi guards asked for the IDs of all the persons in our car, including mine. The trainer submitted his papers to the guards and invented a problem with the guards. He asked to meet the Western official who supervised them.

I knew that the request of the trainer had been accepted when I saw a Western security officer advancing towards us. I could tell his British nationality from his calm accent. He asked us to accompany him to his office. No sooner had we been to the office than the trainer expressed his apologies to the British man.

"We just invented a problem with the guards to meet you," the trainer explained. The trainer ordered me to take the mask off. The problem was over after the British man supervising the guards made sure about my identity. I put on my mask again. We then went out of the office and advanced towards the waiting area.

Working with a Mask on Your Face

A military bus carrying the sign of the Iraqi Security Forces stopped by us. The trainer told me that this was the car that we were waiting for. He added that I should get in this bus with a group of trainers. No sooner had I got into the bus than the trainers asked me to ask the Iraqi soldiers to empty the first four seats in the bus and sit in the back of the bus. The number of soldiers was not more than 25 at that time.

One of the trainers stood by the door of the bus, while another one sat with the other trainers in the front seats. However, they didn't turn their backs to the Iraqi soldiers, but rather aimed their arms towards the soldiers as if they were expecting something from them. The soldiers, on their part, were at their highest alert. I felt myself squeezed between two parties who were about to attack each other. Surely, the trainers had the right to do that because they didn't want to be victims for a terrorist that might have been thrust among those soldiers. The soldiers also had the right to be in such state of expectation, especially when seeing glances of doubt coming out of the trainers' eyes.

During this, I had a different kind of fear and concern that disturbed me. I was scared that one of the soldiers might be living in the same area that I live in, which would expose me and risk the life of my family. That's why, after taking the permission of the senior trainer, I proceeded carefully towards the soldiers and asked them in different pitch and dialect about their residence.

It was a strange feeling to wear a mask. Soldiers were trying to recognize my identity through looking into my eyes, or at least that was my own feeling. I was in the highest state of panic, fearing that one of them could recognize me even if it was only my eyes that appeared for lookers. Praises be to Allah. None of them was living near al-Karakh, but most of them were living near Ar-Rasafa. Every month we receive a group of soldiers from a different Iraqi city.

February 3, 2005

A German Winter in Baghdad

We proceeded to the airport to receive a group of soldiers who were selected to be trained in the camp that I work in. Signs of astonishment and wonder were apparent on the faces of all the soldiers. I didn't know the reason behind that. I felt as if there were many things they wanted to ask about.

As for me, it was strange that the soldiers brought winter clothes, and what is stranger is that some of them put on wool coats while sweat was pouring from their bodies. As a matter of fact the temperature was 60 degrees Celsius in the shade. We were not allowed to join lengthy conversations with the new solders.

Our only mission was to give them directions. Perhaps the officer in charge didn't like their clothing so he took the initiative and asked me, "Are we here in Germany?"

I answered, "Is Germany hot like this?"

It seemed clear that my answer disappointed the guy so he asked me about their residence and if they were still in Iraq. I learned later that their supervisors wanted to keep their training place secret so they told them that they were traveling to Germany. To maintain security measures, they asked the soldiers to call their families to reassure them and not to give them more details about their true destination.

Life in the Camp

Life in the camp is strange to me. It is the first time that I have lived in a completely American environment, which was interesting and hard sometimes because of the differences in culture between me and the American personnel. Besides that, I cannot visit my family although they are only 10 miles away from the camp.

One time I felt that I had to call my mother because I missed her a lot and I did; unfortunately, the area code number showed in her phone and she discovered that I was in Iraq. She asked me to come back home and was emotional, but I convinced her that being in the camp is better for me and much more safe.

17

Love, Chaos and a New Life: February 2005–April 2006

February 3, 2005

Love in the Camp

Days go by; it is all the same. I am working very hard to keep away that sad feeling, which is that of a young man whose dreams are starting to vanish in a country going nowhere. One day my mother called me and asked me to help one of my remote relatives in translation of a military text. My relative is a female who lives in America. She is an American citizen and a single mom. She is a very clever, charming lady and at times we chatted for four hours. Day by day that lady became everything to me.

She is like me in everything. I felt that I had known her a long time ago, even before my first chat with her. She has the same dreams and faith in my country. We decided to meet together in Jordan for the first time. It did not take more than a first meeting in the airport to make our decision that we complete each other. At that meeting was her older brother to help us in completing our marriage contract according to our culture and religion.

June 20, 2005

An Extremist Judge

We went to a judge in Jordan; he was smiling and his face was promising. He asked us where we were from. My wife told him I am

This tank has been creatively painted by a group of kids, an image symbolic of life in Iraq after the invasion.

Kurdish. He started praising Kurds and Salahadding Alaiyobi, the leader who conquered crusaders, and so on; then after this introduction he changed the pattern of his speech completely. He said he was sorry because Kurds marred this entire heritage, which was handed down to them by Salahadding Alaiyobi. They joined crusaders to invade Muslim homelands, indicating the Kurdish alliance with the American forces in the 2003 war.

I was thinking while I listened to the flow of conversation that this judge was an extremist, and he would surely ask me about my lineage. I thought to myself, "If I say to him I'm a Shiite it will be a worse blow, because Shiites joined American forces too"; therefore I decided to conceal this so that the judge would not hamper marriage procedures.

I started to elaborately disparage the Kurds, while my wife giggled with anger. She started disparaging Shiites and how they helped Americans to invade Iraq. This was an assured solution. The judge started looking at me with respect, and soon he asked me about my lineage. I told him I was from Fallujah! He jumped up, he started patting me, and he praised the people of Fallujah and their fight against the American army. Moreover, he agreed on the contract of marriage at once.

Taxi Drivers in Amman

When I rent a taxi and some drivers know that I am an Iraqi, they begin to curse American forces, they describe them with the most hideous characteristics, they praise terrorists in Iraq, and they call them the courageous resistance. My wife used to start defending the U.S. Army and the United States. I was worried that one of the drivers could be one of those extremists and this might endanger my wife's life and her children. Later on, I learned some of them work for the Jordanian intelligence and they want to discover Iraqi terrorists that have migrated to Jordan.

July 20, 2005

The New Baghdad That I Came Back To

I decided to visit my mother before I got my visa entry to America and traveled there. I arrived in Baghdad. The first place that I went to was my friend Diaa's house. Diaa was working with me in the field of human rights. I don't know why Diaa was the first one I decided to visit after such a long time.

Perhaps I did so because I wanted to know of news of Baghdad and the area before going to the house of my family after this long absence. Diaa received me unexpectedly by saying, "Why did you come back?"

I couldn't find an answer because I didn't expect his question and also because I didn't have enough time. He pulled me vigorously into the house. He was confused. He didn't want us to stay too long by the door. I was worried about Diaa's behavior so I asked him, "What's going on? Why are you scared to such an extent? Isn't Baghdad safe as you confirmed to me repeatedly over the phone?" He explained that he just wanted to keep me assured about the safety of my family, no more.

A few minutes later we heard heavy shooting, after which Diaa's face was changed, but he didn't stay in such a state too long. His cellular phone rang and I didn't understand what Diaa said; his short sentences seemed to me meaningless. He was asking the other side about what was going on in the market and if one of them had attacked the market or not. He then hung up and dialed his brother Bahaa, who was working in the nearby market selling amulets. Diaa tried to call Bahaa repeatedly, but in vain.

So he took his revolver and asked me to stay in the house. He told me that he would come back after making sure that his brother was okay. I wasn't able to obey him. I couldn't help myself, hurrying with him towards the nearby market instead. Far from us there were a lot of people grouped. Other groups of the suburb dwellers were running in different directions, carrying arms, while others were carrying women and men who had received gunshot wounds to cars to transport them to the hospital.

Bahaa was among the relievers, screaming, "Where are the police? Where is the American army? Why don't they stop these daily blood baths?" Others kept insulting the followers of Sunni doctrine in general. Diaa didn't notice that I was standing near him. When he noticed me, he asked me to go back to the house quickly. I tried to ask him about the way and about what was going on, but I got no answer. When we reached home, he told me that my coming back is the biggest mistake I have ever made.

"These days Baghdad doesn't know anything but cars hurrying everywhere shooting in all directions," he explained. "Our area comes under armed attack every now and then by a group of armed people in cars who come to the suburb and shower the people with bullets."

My question about the reason was like a question about a complicated philosophical issue. His answer was a sarcastic smile that covered his failure to present reasons. After a long silence he justified that by saying, "Our suburb is inhabited by a Shia majority so Sunni armed men attack the market and spray bullets everywhere to kill the largest concentration of Shia." I felt as if Iraq was going towards an abyss. I wasn't able to think about anything but my family who lived in a nearby suburb, so I proceeded to my house after night had fallen.

I was careful that no one could see me. I hurried to knock on the door quickly, hoping that one of my brothers could open the door before being noticed by our curious neighbor, Om Tarik, who used to pour over me a flood of questions as soon as she saw me till she knew where I was, and why I had disappeared suddenly, though she knew that I had traveled outside Iraq according to the story I told even my family to hide the place that I worked in.

My elder sister opened the door. She was surprised as well as me. She had the very feeling I felt. I felt shocked, seeing her fat and wearing a black dress as if she had become 10 years older. My mother, brothers and sisters gathered around me, embracing me in a way that hardly let me breathe.

I didn't see anything but black color overwhelming the house, in the clothes of my sisters, in their features of their faces that were wondering about a future in which they could see nothing but the blackness of fear and grief. My mother could hardly walk. Her health had deteriorated. My elder sister was widowed because of sectarian violence. Her husband had been killed by a group of Shia extremists just because he was Sunni.

Although I was planning to stay at the house for five days to prepare for my wedding party, the night I spent in our front garden outside the prison-like house got me frustrated from the news of murdered and dead people among my family and in my suburb where I live, not to mention the murder of my kind brother-in-law, two uncles, and two cousins. Also I knew that my brother Mazin had left the suburb where a Sunni majority used to live. He was obliged to escape with his family at night, carrying nothing but their own clothes.

I felt choked inside the house and I longed for fresh air away from the smell of blood in Baghdad. The only thing that drew me back to our family prison cell, our house, was the begging of my mother to come in and not to stay in the garden, in order to avoid the bullets of a Sunni sniper that might be lurking somewhere in the neighboring Sunni suburb. This suburb had never been a sectarian suburb but it had become the rule in Baghdad that the suburbs with a Sunni majority should be controlled by Sunni militia that expel Shia and vice versa.

Our suburb became for Shia only. Even my Sunni friends stopped visiting me because they were afraid they would be killed. I stayed awake that night, thinking about my city, homeland, family and the dreams of stability, prosperity and freedom that I hoped to see come to reality after the fall of Saddam Hussein's regime. Is this really the end of all good hopes and the beginning of more misery and black dresses to be worn by little girls in Iraq 50 years from now?

I wasn't able to stay in Baghdad anymore. It was not the old Baghdad. Even mornings had become heavy, gloomy and frightening for some Iraqi women, who didn't expect their husbands, brothers and children to come back again after leaving the house. I decided to gather my clothes in my bag and tell my family that I was traveling again but with no return this time.

The begging of my elder sister didn't work this time to keep me a few days. My mother was like a mute, who couldn't express her confusion. She was torn between two thoughts: to let me travel, with only Allah knowing if we would meet again; or to let me stay, where one morning she might hurry to the house door after hearing the sound of shooting, to find me bloodstained. Death has become the most expected thing in Baghdad. Death became the rule, while safety, life and peace have become the exceptions.

When I intended to leave, or rather escape, I didn't think of it as an escape from death, but an escape from being killed near my mother. I was afraid that my mother would find me, at the end of her life, a victim covered with newspapers and thrown in one of the Baghdad streets. They stole my beautiful Baghdad and colored it with blood. In the taxi taking me back to Arbeel, along a highway with fences destroyed by American tanks that were trying to escape the terrorists, I didn't notice anything but holes caused by bombs on both sides of the road. It seemed as if it had been part of a fierce battle.

Everything was gloomy in my city including people, streets and even the sky. While I was absorbed in thinking, I was scared by the sight of a man killed inside his car at the side of the road. I was more scared by the people passing by the killed man. They showed no reaction, perhaps because murder was usual, or because they had been killed from inside and had become dead bodies moving in the streets. The taxi driver was listening to a sad song in the cassette. The song affected me and I burst into tears, which obliged the taxi driver to turn off the cassette, but I asked him to pay no attention and to reopen the tape player again and repeat the song so that my tears could take out some of my sorrows.

Flee to Heaven

The American embassy in Jordan is very crowded with those who apply for emigration visas, especially with Iraqis who are working with the American army, and American companies working in Iraq. I found many Iraqi female translators, among them Nada, who was with an aged American man.

She was applying to travel to America, because she is married to this man, regardless of the huge differences between them. She is in her twenties and he is in his sixties; in addition, she was a Muslim and he apparently was Christian.

The Islam religion does not allow a Muslim woman to marry a Christian. This made him change his religion in the front of the Jordanian courts to accept the marriage agreement. I was standing in a line, a long line, to reach the American embassy guards, the majority of whom are Jordanian; they treated my wife and me differently.

The difference in the way they talked to her and the way they treated me was the difference between my green, cheap paper Iraqi passport, and the blue, excellent paper passport of my wife. Supposedly, a man asks for his wife's rights and protects her from any violation of her rights. As to me, the other way around is right. The American passport of my wife adds a kind of humanity, respect, and duty to their treatment of me. In my second visit, my wife was not with me. This meant I was without any security cover and that I shifted, after being a man married to a lady from the First World, to a being from the Third World according to the classification applied outside the fence of the American embassy.

I sighed deeply while entering the American embassy. This is the embassy of the country which protects human rights. Nobody mistreated me inside it. I was not afraid to say that I was a translator with the American forces in Iraq, or that is what I thought. When I came close to a Jordanian official, working at the American embassy, when he took my papers, his face turned pale. He asked me about my job. I told him proudly, "I work with Americans in Iraq."

He said, "Are you working with those who occupied your country?"

At that time, I asked myself, has the picture of America become negative even at an institution of its own?

Elections

I was waiting for the visa to travel to the U.S. The region of al-Lwebda mountain in Amman looks active with the movement of runaway Iraqis from Baghdad to there. Today is the day of Iraqi elections: secular list, Sunni list, and Shiite list. The Sunni list's agenda looks restricted to defending the rights of Sunnis only, and the Shiite list looks the same too, to defend the rights of Shiites only.

The secular list defends every person who does not find his interests in the other lists, especially some members of the Ba'ath party, which used to control Iraq during Saddam Hussein's reign, and whose members have lost their advantages and privileges. I did not find myself in any of these lists; therefore I changed my mind at the door of the polling center. I went back to my apartment without having selected any of the sectarian lists.

November 9, 2005

Amman Explosions

I went to the supermarket close by the apartment where I live in Amman. I wanted to buy some canned food and fresh food. The owner of the supermarket was an old man; we were acquaintances because of my frequent visits to his shop. When he saw me, he asked me to take the canned food and go back home as soon as possible and stay there. When I asked why, he told me there were Iraqi terrorists who had bombed a hotel in Jordan. I was astonished at what he said. I asked him, "Why do I have to stay at my apartment? What do I have to do with all this?"

He told me that the Jordanians are very angry; they are attacking any Iraqis on the streets and beating them up just because they are Iraqis. I have no choice but to take the canned food and go back to the apartment quickly. I have to stay in this apartment and between these walls for a long time. Indeed my friend who resides in Amman at a quarter in the middle of the city told me that Iraqis are being beaten up and humiliated in the streets of the Jordanian capital this evening. The Iraqi wandering vendors disappeared from the commercial area of town because of the violence reaching them. I decided not to leave the apartment until I go to the American embassy when they call me and finish my immigration papers.

When the Fire Comes Close to Your House

The point of view of Amman people changed after the terrorist event, which reached a hotel and changed the wedding party of a young man and woman to a funereal one. Some of the bride and groom's people were killed in addition to a number of attendants. The people of Amman realized that terrorism in Iraq is not too far to reach them too.

February 22, 2006

Blowup of the Golden Dome

I have been trying to call my family since this morning but in vain. It looks as though the government stopped communication services between Iraq and the rest of the world's countries in an attempt to control the sectarian violence which invaded Iraqi cities, especially Baghdad.

The Golden Dome in Samarra was not just a dome for a place where Shiites worship; it had much larger implications. It represented the highest holiness and respect for the followers of Shiite doctrine. This is the reason behind the terrorists' aiming at it.

It is the red line, which nobody may cross, because the Shiites' fire will burn everything if that holy symbol is harmed.

If the terrorists want to pull Shiites into a sectarian war with Sunnis, they have to cause harm to Shiites beyond killing the followers of Shiite teaching. Shiites do not care for life as much as they care for those golden domes in Samara, Baghdad, Najaf, and Karbala.

Al-Qaida and the Golden Dome

Anyone who examines carefully the policies of the terrorist al-Qaida organization in Afghanistan will see that it is based on differentiation between Shiites and Sunnis for two reasons. First, the Shiites are the conventional enemy of the Wahabi concept adopted by al-Qaida. Second, al-Qaida needs a foothold in any region to stay there, because it is not from that region, but is a group of terrorists from different nationalities joining the same sick belief.

In addition, it cannot find an excuse to stay in this country or that without convincing one of the parties that it would be a strong ally to fight the other party, especially with the financial angle where hundreds of millions of Gulf dollars flow to this organization. At the end, al-Qaida joins the party closest to its belief; in Iraq it is Sunnis, because they do not consider the al-Wahabi concept contradicting with them and they accept it sometimes.

Here we have to differentiate between al-Wahabi concept and al-Qaida; all al-Wahabi followers are not al-Qaida allies. To apply this norm in Iraq, al-Qaida aimed at Shiites only to pull them into a civil war with Sunnis. It convinced some Sunnis that by aiming at Shiites it is trying to impose the terms of Sunnis and protect their interests.

Many times, it attempted this and aimed at big Shiite gatherings, but in vain. Mr. Sistani, the highest Shiite authority, declared that he is against the fighting of Iraqis against each other despite their beliefs and religion. It is known that Shiites cannot disagree with their high authorities. Al-Qaida realized that, therefore it strived to provoke the extremist party in Iraqi Shiites, who are the followers of Muqtada al-Sadr. They blew up the Golden Dome, which is regarded as one of the greatest holies for Shiites. This pushed the ignorant among the followers of al-Sadr to respond with killing and burning, and more than this, they began to harm mosques of Sunnis, forgetting that these are God's homes and they are nobody else's.

After I called my family, I called my friend to assure him as well; he was very frustrated and sad at the situation of human rights going towards the abyss. Killing and displacement because of race cannot be compared to anything. He was very worried; he told me that Mahdi army militia had begun to recruit Shiite youth in his quarter. They have begun to convince them that they are fighting to protect them and their families, especially after the bombing of the Golden Dome in Samarra and after Sunnis began to retaliate against the killing and displacement done to them and against the ruin of their mosques.

The Iraqi and Arabic television channels have begun to increase the sectarian hate charges. All are heading towards a sectarian war. My answer to this is that sectarian war between Iraqis is impossible. They have lived together for hundreds of years, loving each other and united despite the racial and ideological differences. My friend who was at the actual site answered me mockingly, saying that the good Iraqis do not start the sectarian war, but are pulled into it by groups of this faction or that. These groups have specific political agendas pushed from outside to block the democratic process in Iraq.

What shocked me and increased my worries and concern about the future of Iraq is that, he told me, the Shiite militias have begun to recruit thieves and murderers in the neighborhood, among whom is Muhammad who became a leader in the Mahdi army, and who was just a gang member stealing cars and killing their drivers. My country and its future is in the hands of a group of ignorant killers and robbers. The voice of Sistani al-Hakeem calls on everyone to stop those who want to harm Iraq, but this call is not heard by many people. When the voice of bullets rises up the voice of reason is not heard.

Many Small Baghdads

All this is happening in our city, which has been divided into regions of Shiite advantage and others of Sunni. This led to an increase in divorce cases among Shiite-Sunni married couples. Many families whose parents are from different ideologies have dissolved and disappeared. The Sunni militia forced men who were married to Shiite women to divorce them; otherwise they either get killed or are forced to leave the Sunni district. The same thing is true with regard to Shiite militia.

My sister had to leave Iraq with her husband, in order to keep her family safe. Because her husband is Sunni she cannot stay at her home with him, since the district came under the control of Sunni extremists.

As for my other siblings, they lost their jobs. My older sister could not go to work a month ago, because although her work is in Bablmua'd-ham, which is controlled by Shiite militia, to get there she must pass through districts under the control of Sunnis. Of course, there are men wearing Iraqi police uniform. They establish bogus checkpoints. They stop cars passing by. They make the passengers get out.

If the bogus checkpoint belongs to Sunni extremists, they will ask for passengers' identification cards. Depending on the last name and the name of the tribe, they recognize their sect. They capture Shiites and they execute them immediately. Shiite extremists do the same. If you have no identification with you, you are dead immediately. They will ask you to say the declaration, "There is no god but Allah and Mohammed is messenger of God." This is for Sunnis. Shiites add this to it: "Ali is saint of God."

If you mention the Shiites' declaration and you are at a Sunni checkpoint, you will be killed. If you just say the Sunni declaration and you are at a Shiite checkpoint, you will be killed. It depends on your luck. You do not know who will stop you, or to which sect the checkpoint belongs. My sister told me a checkpoint stopped her with her girlfriend, but her girlfriend did not have an identification card with her, so she said she was dumb. She escaped death miraculously.

The Peaceful Lack Peace

There are few families remaining in our street. All Sunnis were driven away from our district. al-Mahdi militia took over the whole district. The government disappeared from the scene completely; the militia were from Shiite extremists. On the other side, Sunni extremists took over the district opposite to our district, which is separated from our district only by the main street, where all businesses were closed. The street on which these business are located became the contact line separating fighting militia.

The violence in our district did not extend to Sunnis only, but to the Christians also. Some of them were killed, and the rest traveled either to the north of Iraq where some Christian villages are or outside Iraq to neighboring countries such as Jordan and Syria, to escape death. The reason for driving away the Christians is that the Mahdi army militia wants to take over the market for alcoholic beverages in the district. The law gives the right of selling alcoholic beverages to Christians, and the Shiite extremists want to benefit from this trade without selling alcoholic beverages openly, as they claim to commit to Islam, which outlaws alcoholic beverages.

The Shiite militia threatened Christians in our district who were working in the alcoholic beverage trade, and they burnt the businesses of those who refused to obey the new leaders of Iraq, but only after they had looted it to sell it later on the black market.

My Nephew's Meal

Whenever I call my mother, despite all of this, she tells me that she lives in the district with peace and security everywhere so that I do not get worried about her and the rest of my siblings. But I know the

Two men take shelter under a makeshift tent, with a mosque in the background.

truth over the phone from my talkative youngest sister. I also ask to talk to my young nephews and I get information from them. My brother Ahmed's daughter told me she is hungry. When I asked her about the reason, she told me that they have not gone shopping for twenty days. This has made my mother decrease the meals to just a sufficient amount to keep them alive. She does not want to use up the saved food, because there are Sunni snipers on the building overlooking the main street. Because our house is close to the main street, the house's gate and the palm trees in our garden get the greatest number of shots.

Telephone Call

Telephone calls are a heavy burden for me, especially those calls I receive after midnight from family in Iraq. With each phone ring, countless fears jump into my mind: these cold wires may convey to me the bad news of the killing of one of my brothers or perhaps the kidnapping of another. It is an endless series of frightening expectations that worry any Iraqi immigrant. This is why I avoid calling my family too, which causes my mother grief sometimes.

Sympathizing with my mother, my wife urges me to call them every time she hears news of bombing or terrorist operations in Iraq. For a time I ignored that and didn't call. This obliged my wife to call them and ask them to call me to embarrass me so that I would speak to them. Sometimes I wasn't able to call them because of the poor phone lines in Baghdad. I tried to call all the phones of my brothers but in vain. This made me more scared and more worried about them. I was afraid that something bad might have happened to one of them.

Today and after repeated trials to call my family, I was able to reach my younger sister, who is only 24 years old. She spoke to me in defeated language and a faint voice. I insisted that she should tell me what worried her and if something bad had happened to my brothers and mother. She was obliged to swear many times that nothing bad had happened to the family, but she suffered certain pressures at her work. I wanted to help her by giving advice on how to deal with the work pressures, but she laughed and said, "My work pressures are different than any work pressures you may think of and so nobody can help me."

My small young sister, who graduated from college two years ago and registered to obtain an MA degree, works now in the analysis laboratory in one of the Baghdad hospitals. I thought this success in her scientific life would give her some happiness, especially when achieving her dream by obtaining the MA degree. The truth is that her nerves can't bear the things that she sees for six hours every day. She is in charge of supervising the storing of dead bodies in the hospital freezer, and preserving the corpses from decay. Most of the bodies had their heads missing.

No sooner had she started telling me the details of her work than she started weeping. She described the procedures of storing dead bodies. She starts her working day at 8 in the morning with a daily workload of not fewer than 100 dead bodies stacked before the freezer, waiting for the start of the shift. She starts her work by receiving the bodies. Most of the bodies have been tied up from behind and shot in the chest. Most of the bodies are without heads. Signs of torture can be seen on the entire body. She works with a man in his middle forties. He works on pulling the bodies inside the freezer.

"When he comes late, he waves for me so that I walk quietly among dead bodies and avoid stepping on the arm or leg of anybody. I do that till I reach my office," she complained. "A more terrible thing is that the freezer can't accommodate the dead bodies that arrive daily. The freezer receives 100 bodies daily; most of them are unidentified, which means that nobody claimed to know them, not to mention the other bodies that reached the freezer in the previous days without identifying or burying them," she added.

This forced my sister to alternate the dead bodies outside the freezer with those inside the freezer so that each group stays one day inside, and another day outside. This preserves the temperature of all the bodies, and prevents their decay. Unfortunately, this doesn't work all the time, which obliges her to take photos of bodies before submitting them to the government to bury them. She keeps the photos to provide them for families looking for their missing sons. This works only if the family was lucky enough to find the body with his head still on.

April 12, 2006

A Middle Eastern Trip

Looking at the walls of my house in Amman with my immigration papers in the bag in my right hand, I wondered if this would be my last trip, after which I would never travel again. This came to mind after getting used to long years of continuous travel among different countries.

I got used also to different kinds of travel such as traveling between myself and my dreams. I had to submit the papers to the nearest American immigration department. The KLM plane took off and flew all night above the Mediterranean. After long hours, I reached the Amsterdam Airport, where I spent a few hours waiting for the other American Northwest plane.

Do They Deserve to Be Cursed?

I stopped by a coffee shop to drink coffee in the airport. There was a man standing behind me. Maybe out of curiosity he talked to me, because he noticed I was talking to an Arab standing close by me, in a language that did not sound like Spanish. When someone sees me he thinks right away I speak it; I do not know why. He hurried to ask me about my country. I told him I am from Iraq.

This increased his curiosity; he invited me to drink coffee with him to talk about what is going on in Iraq. While we were waiting for our plane, I accepted his invitation. When we sat down as he talked to me, he asked me about what I felt during the war. I explained to him I was waiting for American forces to enter Baghdad as soon as possible, to save us from a dictator's regime. In addition, how I was in the Iraqi army, and how the American fighters were bombing our locations. I wished to stay alive to enjoy freedom after the war.

When I talked to the guy about war victims, his eyes started to shine like a shark's eyes. He asked me to explain the scenes of death in detail, especially scenes of American rocket explosions and dead bodies of Iraqi soldiers. He seemed like a shark following the red lines of blood of its prey in the water. I explained to him that war, any war, cannot happen without the death of innocent victims, even if the war was for a noble goal such the American war with Iraq, which I believe is a noble war despite the different points of view about its legality and the reasons why it happened. Its important result is the overthrow of a dictator regime.

The man shocked me when he said, "Did the American planes kill many of you and cut their bodies?"

He was smiling as he said it, asking me to explain to him how my fellow soldiers in the army bled to death. I felt that the person was not normal and was psychologically sick. Therefore, I got up and left the coffee shop. I am for the war to get rid of Saddam Hussein, but I'm against viewing Iraqi soldiers as enemies who deserve to be cut and killed, simply because they have to stay in the front so they will be not executed by Iraqi forces.

Therefore, they stayed neutral at their fighting locations. They did not fight Americans. I think some civilians do not understand this, contrary to the American army, which treated us according to this neutral stance. This explains why the American fighters did not aim at the Iraqi soldiers except in unusual cases and after giving warnings.

Amsterdam Airport:
Peace Is a Dream, It Needs Courage

I advanced with pride and I saluted her; she was an Israeli in her forties, sitting and waiting for her flight. I have outrun for the third time the Arabic press, with its lies and the control it has had over our brains for decades, portraying Israelis as enemies.

The first time was at Almustansiriya University in Baghdad, when I accompanied an old Jewish man, who was in a delegation from the West, which has visited Iraq to lift the economic sanctions. I remember at that time the discussions that took place between me and some students who treated me roughly and chided me, because I was walking and talking to that Jewish man, and how the students were saying that the Jews are our permanent enemies.

My answer to them was that man is man regardless of anything. He deserves love and respect. This is contrary to what the Iraqi government did in the midst of the last century, when they killed Jews and imprisoned some of them, and looted their money with no right. What I have said made Farah Philip, a Christian student, cry when she heard it. She told me how her Jewish grandma was forced to change her religion to Christianity to remain in Iraq, otherwise she would have to migrate to Israel.

The second time was in Jordan, when I met a girl called Nikola; she was a Jew from Germany, an activist in the field of human rights. At the time we were in a restaurant in Amman, and the atmosphere was very friendly around her. All the guys around her admired her personality and her beauty and they tried to get close to her. The discussion was going in this pattern until Nikola said she wanted to travel to Jerusalem.

The friendly atmosphere around her changed to an atmosphere full of suspicion, distrust and fear. My friend Ali, an activist in the field of human rights, asked her about the reason for traveling to Israel, hardly swallowing his saliva. All the youths who used to admire her shut up and leaned against the back of their chairs keeping away from her.

Nikola said honestly, "I am an Israeli!" Within two minutes all the youths left the table, under different excuses.

She felt it but she did not know the reason. When she asked me I laughed bitterly and I told her that they still were living according to the lies of the Arabic press. They run away and avoid getting close to or talking to any Israeli, because the Arabic press imagines that any friendly talks between Arabs and Israelites are an Israeli attempt to recruit Arabs to work against their countries. It requires courage and sound thinking to overreach this, in addition to a complete faith in the ability of Arabs and Israelis to make peace.

A Middle Eastern Smile

A U.S. plane had to take me to Sea-Tac Airport in Washington State. I was finally in America. I thought well of myself and every other smiling person, but after noticing the way that others were looking at

A typical military checkpoint manned by American soldiers.

me in the airport, I found it necessary to expand the area of the smile on my face. All looked at me as if I was a suspect, especially after I stood in line in front of the terminal.

One of the guards asked me, "Where are you going and where did you come from?"

"I'm coming from Iraq and going to the United States of America," I answered.

Of course, and as usual in all Western airports that I visited, one of the airport guards preceded towards me and said, "You have been randomly selected to get additional inspection."

No sooner had I stood in the inspection line than I found myself laughing upon seeing some old ladies looking anxiously at me and thankfully to the airport guard. They looked at the guard proudly and gratefully as if they wanted to say, "You did well by catching him."

Unfortunately, their gladness didn't last for too long after the guard let me pass to the terminal. As a matter of fact, this was not the end of the story. They called my name over the microphone, and one of the officials asked me to change my place inside the plane, claiming that a family would like to sit together in one place. This led me to sit near a guard who was disguised in normal clothes. That was clear from his figure and kind of pants. He was wearing the kind of pants that security guards used to wear. It seems that the image of the man coming from the Middle East became very bad, even when he had the biggest smile in the world.

April 13, 2006

Last Dream

On the stairs of the airplane I was trying to get down, a blond stewardess smiled in my face and said, "Welcome to America."

Upon waking I asked myself, "Is there a day I will hear an Iraqi stewardess telling me, "Welcome to Iraq?"

Index

Al- entries are alphabetized under the primary word.

193